NOVEL BASICS

An Illustrated Guide to Writing a Novel

JULIET KINCAID

Juliet Kincaid
AzureSky Press, LLC
P. O. Box 4214
Overland Park, KS 66204

Copyright @ 2018
ISBN: 9781730833991

Cover art and design by Juliet Kincaid

Dedication

To my students . . .
You have taught me so much.

NOVEL BASICS
An Illustrated Guide to Writing a Novel

Introduction

I know you're out there. I've met you in some way or another.

Maybe you're the unconfident young woman in an online group I belong to who wants to start your coming-of-age novel about growing up in the Ozarks amid the opioid crisis, but you don't quite know how to do that.

You could be a short story writer intimidated by the sheer size of a novel.

Or maybe you're the man I talked to at a local authors fair who always meant to get back to that novel you started twenty years ago, but now it sits hidden in a drawer at home.

Perhaps you tried to write a 50,000-word novel during a National Novel Writing Month event, but you didn't make it all the way through.

Or you did finish and now you have the diploma declaring you a NaNoWriMo winner, but you don't know what to do next.

Let's say that you're the author of a brilliant, well-received first novel who can't get that sophomore effort together.

You could be a best-selling author on a tight schedule who needs to get cracking on the next book in your series.

Or you're the author of a best-selling series for which you still have a ton of ideas, but a notion for a brand new book or series has crept into your head, and it's so strong that it wakes you up in the middle of the night. Still, before you commit, you'd like to explore it.

Maybe you're writing a nonfiction book about yourself growing up or a shocking event that happened in your hometown, but you're thinking the book might be better as a novel, so you can distance yourself from the material emotionally and have more latitude with facts.

Maybe you're like me. You have several completed novels in your file cabinet that you could never get an agent or publisher interested in, so you gave up on those projects. Possibly taking a little time to explore one of those will help you decide if it's worthwhile for you to go back to it.

Or maybe you don't fit into any of these slots I've mentioned, but still you're like the rest of us. You've got an idea sparked by that powerful question "What if?" that keeps bugging you, an itch you'd like to scratch at least a little bit.

Maybe you're not a writer. Instead, you're an avid fiction reader who would like to learn more about the novel so you can sharpen your insights into the selections you discuss at your book club.

Regardless, I'm thinking that my method using twenty 3" by 5" index cards will help you to brainstorm your novel or study someone else's.

But before I start guiding you through the process of

creating your own pack of twenty cards, I'd like to share some of my history with the novel and thus establish some credentials to write this book. (If you're impatient to get to the cards, please skip this part and go to the page break.)

As for my personal experiences with the novel, I don't remember learning to read in the first place, and I don't recall the first novel I read. Reading novels was just something I did along with Dad, Mom and my older brother Dale. Much later in our lives, Dale used to call me, and we'd chat for a half hour or so about the latest thrillers we'd read recently. As an old Navy man, my brother loved Tom Clancy's books. I kept up with John Grisham. When I was a kid, Dad loved C. S. Forester's Horatio Hornblower novels so much that he took up model ship making. My mom read historical romances, the sort with a bare-chested guy and a semi-bare-breasted gal embracing on the cover.

In fact, the summer before I turned eleven, I took one of Mom's books over to the schoolyard across the alley from where we lived. Sitting on a step in the shade, I was deep into reading the novel when a counselor for the summer playground program found me. A stocky woman who wore khaki shorts and a camp shirt, she asked, "Should you be reading that?"

"Sure," I said. "Why not?" And, undeterred, I kept on reading and reading and reading novels.

In Fifth Grade, I came in second in a contest our teacher held. The winner read more books–Little Golden Books. I read fewer books, but lots more pages.

My favorites back then usually involved action and adventure in places distant from my hometown of Huntington, WV. These included Rudyard Kipling's *Kim* set in faraway, fabulous India and Andre Norton's *Scarface*, a historical YA novel about a kid abducted by pirates in the Caribbean. I also enjoyed Frances Hodgson Burnett's *The Secret Garden*.

In the long ago summers of my youth, I went to the Carnegie library once a week on Mondays to return the six novels I read the week before and to check out six more.

The summer before I turned fifteen, I began keeping a record of the books I'd read. The first entry was *The Saint on the Spanish Main* by Leslie Charteris. Mystery! Adventure! I loved that kind of escapist fare when I was a kid, and I still do. More than forty years after I started my life list of the books I've read, I formed the ambition to read three thousand novels before I kick the bucket. But when I went back to my card file to see how many books I had to go, I discovered I'd already passed my goal by a hundred and sixty-four books. True, not all the books I read were novels and some novels I'd read more than once, but still, I figured I'd reached my goal. Who knows? If I live long enough, maybe I'll read another thousand.

An aside . . . Lots of writers were scribblers when they were kids. Not me. Writing was something I did for school. What I was becoming was an English major, long before I even knew what that was. I didn't start writing fiction until I went to graduate school for my doctorate. Whenever I took a seminar, I wrote a paper for the class and a story to share with my friends. (We especially got a giggle out of my novella called "Graduate Student Blues" that satirized the pompous professor of a course we all had to take to get our degrees.) I also wrote my first novel in graduate school as a way of exploring the subject of my dissertation: fiction in diary form.

(By the way, my students at one of America's finest community colleges used to call me Dr. J. I'm not nearly as tall as Julius Erving, the basketball-playing Dr. J, but my Ph. D. entitles me to the nickname. If you like, you can call me that, too.)

Since then, I've written about fifty more short stories and about a dozen novels. To date, I've self-published around twenty individual short stories, four short story collections, and five novels.

This just about brings me up to date. As for my future, I can pretty much predict what at least one part of it looks like since there's nothing that I love more than going inside a big novel, slamming the door behind me to shut out this fractious world, and living in an imagined world with a clever hero for a while. Because I mostly read in bed at night and barring my getting run down by a bus, I suspect that when I do kick the bucket, whoever finds my mortal remains will have to pry a novel from my cold dead hands.

Maybe it will be the novel you've written.

<> <> <>

Creating your personalized deck of twenty cards that will help you explore your novel won't take long, probably at most a couple of hours–including a break in the middle when your fitness tracker prompts you to get up from your desk or table and dash around your office, your apartment, or your favorite coffeehouse. The place doesn't matter much as long as you can count on two hours of almost uninterrupted time.

Stop! Stop! Stop! Hold your horses here!

After I thought I'd finished this introduction and was ready to move on to the discussion of the first card you'll make, I had an epiphany. (That's something I love about writing. By writing, you learn lessons you never realized you didn't know but needed to.)

Back to my epiphany . . .

Taking my Novel Basics class in a physical classroom with me in charge of the proceedings and limited time to provide examples and for my students to create their personalized packs of cards is different from your reading the first part of this book and going through the process with unlimited time available to you.

So I'll leave it up to you to decide how much time to take to create your set of cards. Still, I think it might be good to jot down the numbers, names, and questions fast. I use the blank sides of the cards for this part of the process because the images look better on them. But though the pictures are fun, they're optional.

At this point, the answers on the other sides of the cards are optional as well. If you know the answer to the question a card asks right away, that's fine. Jot it down. If you don't, move on. If you sit there and stew, you might not get your cards done.

Indeed, you might not even start. One time I served as a guinea pig for an art therapy session. We used 2½" by 3¾" cards instead of 3" by 5", but the concept was the same–to get through them as fast as we could. As I merrily collaged card after card, I looked over to see a woman so paralyzed by self-doubt and fear of failure and her creativity so wounded that she wrung her hands over the first card, still blank. This makes me want to cry for her.

Maybe something like that happened to that novel some of you always meant to start or write or finish. How did that happen? It's really simple, I suspect. You let your ump out and that shut up your imp.

Ump? Imp? What are you talking about now, Dr. J? you might ask.

It goes back to the left-brain, right-brain theory of how our mental processes work and the attachment of the label *left-brained* to someone who tends to be logical and critical and *right-brained* to someone who tends to be creative and imaginative. I call the former voice in my head my ump and the latter voice my imp.

Definition of *ump*: the critic, the perfectionist, the logician who lives on the left side of your head, the

English teacher of everybody's nightmares who says, "If you don't get this absolutely perfect the first time through, you might as well not start at all."

Definition of *imp*: the energy, the source, the little kid who lives on the right side of your brain, jumps up and down, waves an imaginary hand to get your attention, and says, "I got an idea. I got an idea."

In essence, writing isn't a left-brained activity. It isn't solely a right-brained activity either. It's a whole-brained process. To write anything including a novel–maybe especially a novel–you need both your ump and your imp.

But if you let your ump shoot its mouth off too early in the process, you will completely demoralize your imp. And it will quit talking to you altogether and curl up into a small, tight fetal ball.

So when your ump starts saying to you, "Wait! Wait! That's not exactly the word you need"; or "Is that the correct *there, their, they're*?"; or "Why bother? It will never sell"; just say, "Yeah, yeah, yeah, button it, Ump. You'll get your chance later." And then, coax your imp to come out and play.

We are not after perfection here. We're looking for the basics you need to know about your novel before you start to write it, or most of the basics anyway. For example, you might not come up with all the major characters the first time through your cards. Probably you won't know all of the characters' names. You might not answer all the questions. It's not as if you have to show your work to anybody. So relax and enjoy the process.

Telling your ump to cool it goes for drawing the images on your cards, too, if you decide to do them at all. Some of the images on my deck of cards are really messy. And I simply don't care.

Okay, to get back to the subject of this section . . . To brainstorm your novel, you need something to write on, specifically twenty 3" by 5" index cards, and a pen or pencil to write with. (Line up two to four in case one breaks.)

As I said, I put the numbers, names, questions and images on the blank sides of cards and save the lined sides for my answers and specific notes. But you do whatever works for you.

I also enjoy color, so I used a variety of colors of cards and different colors of pens, too. And no, there is absolutely no system or coding to the colors of the cards I used. The very idea of doing that makes my brain seize up. So if you prefer to put everything down in black and white on 3" x 5" cards that are blank on both sides, make it so.

From my experience with the Novel Basics process in a classroom, it takes a really tight hour just busting along or a slightly more leisurely ninety minutes to create your personalized pack of cards. But even though you, my dear reader and fellow novelist, aren't in a physical classroom with me, I suggest that you hustle.

I'm excited about getting started, and I hope you are,

too. We are going to have so much fun. So let's begin.

P. S. If you're a reader who has no interest in writing a novel, you might want to ask and answer the questions as they relate to a novel you've read and admired. But I warn you. You very well might catch the novel-writing bug.

PART 1: Brainstorm Your Novel

How to Brainstorm a Novel
With Twenty 3" by 5" Cards

The Heart Card

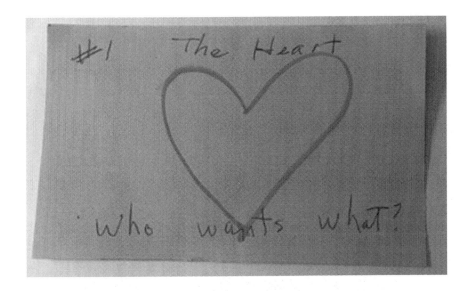

**The Heart Card asks the question,
"Who wants what?"**

At the heart of every novel–every story really, no matter the form it takes, novel, short story, play, movie or television script, or epic narrative poem for that matter–lies the question, "Who wants what?"

As like as not, what you write down on Card # 1, with only a vague notion of what your novel will be, won't be very specific. You probably don't have a name for *the who*, for instance. Your answer might be something not much more than the following:

Boy wants girl.

Girl wants boy.

Boy wants boy.

Girl wants girl.

Even more broadly, someone wants to find true love.

More specifically, a returning veteran named Jay Gatsby wants to find Daisy, the girl he left behind, and make her his own.

Let's move on to other genres besides love stories . . .

In murder mysteries the detective wants to find the killer to keep her from doing it again and/or to bring her to justice.

Someone wants to escape something, his hometown for instance, or her abusive mother for another.

Someone wants to find something, the Holy Grail, a magical ring, or the owner of a lost dog.

Someone wants to get rich.

Katniss Everdeen wants to save her little sister Prim from the Hunger Games.

Minty Wilcox, the protagonist of *January Jinx*, the first novel in my Calendar Mystery series, wants to find a job as a typist/stenographer in Kansas City in 1899.

Often in fiction, as in life, a want becomes a need. Someone needs to find a job to stay alive. The Chosen One needs to save Middle Earth, the world, or the galaxy before he and everyone he knows perish.

Regardless, to start a novel you need to know what

someone wants or needs to accomplish by the last page of the narrative. Or at the very least you need to have a general idea of who wants want in your novel. To put it in literary terms, **a story needs a protagonist with whom the reader can willingly identify and who has a worthwhile goal.**

I put that in bold because it's important, but I'm not going into it right now. We'll talk about that when we get to Card # 3.

Card # 3? What happened to Card # 2?

I'm so glad you asked.

Card # 2
The Outcome Card

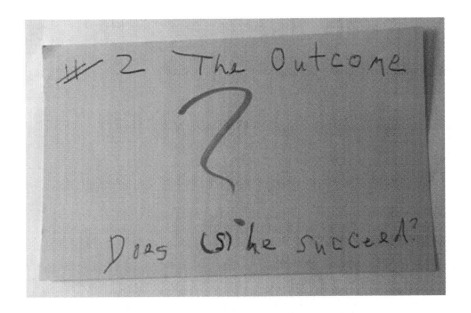

The Outcome Card asks the question, "Does (s)he succeed?"

In answering the question on the second card, "Does she or he succeed?" you will figure out if *the who* gets what she wants or needs. Or more formally, does the protagonist accomplish his goal by the end of the novel?

Let me explain through an analogy. Writing a novel is a trip, and it won't be a short one like bopping over to the closest QuikTrip to gas up the truck–unless of course the floodwaters are approaching and your protagonist named George must get enough gas not only for the truck but also for the generator back at the house so he doesn't lose all the frozen food in the freezer during the inevitable power outage. And that way, his family of five including newborn twins . . . Oh, I do so love to write fiction, but let's press on.

Writing a novel is a long and maybe even an emotionally arduous and physically challenging journey. So it's good to know where you're headed when you start out, so you don't get lost along the way and end up making lots of little side trips that take you nowhere.

To use another analogy entirely . . . Writing a novel is like walking on a tightrope. It really helps if you have the far side of the narrative tethered to something before you start out, if not to a specific rock or tree over there, at least in the general neighborhood of where you want to be at the end.

Besides these reservations, knowing where you're going lets you know what kind of journey you'll make and allows you to plan the journey.

We'll go into those issues later, but now, you should write *yes* or *no* on the back of your 3" by 5" card.

Let's go back to the "girl wants boy" and "boy wants girl" examples we talked about for the heart card.

Yes, of course, Cinderella gets Prince Charming.

The Star Card

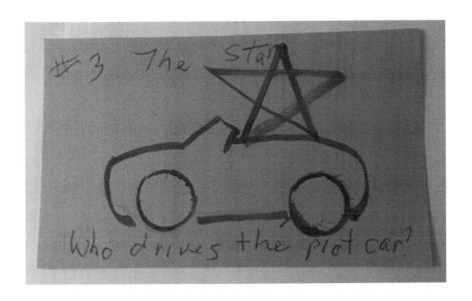

The Star Card asks the question,
"Who drives the plot car?"

On Card # 3, you'll jot down a few details about who will star in your novel, that is, the kind of person in the leading role. I put the star inside a car because it's very important that your main character, aka your protagonist, generally drives the plot of your novel and makes its actions happen, especially as he or she nears the end of the journey.

You might not know this character's name yet, but probably you can already make some basic decisions about this character. Will your protagonist be male or female?

How old is your protagonist?

Another thing you might want to explore on your third card–at least a little bit at this point–is **why** your protagonist wants to accomplish the particular goal that you've given that character. To save a life? His own or someone else's? To prove herself? To clear his name, or her sister's or his brother's? To solve the crime and thus keep the murderer from killing more people? Why does Gatsby want Daisy? That question is so easy to answer. The poor guy loves her.

Another thing to think about even at this early stage of brainstorming your novel: what about the star of the novel keeps her from accomplishing her goal and your novel from reaching its outcome right away? He can't be perfect. None of us are. Besides, perfection is boring. Even Superman has his Kryptonite. Something internal like self-doubt might hold your protagonist back or something external like a broken leg when she's out in a blizzard.

Tip: avoid putting a complete schmuck in the driver's seat of your plot car. It makes most readers uncomfortable to be forced to identify with someone capable of the worst villainy without any redeeming virtues at all, an all-powerful being who, for example, wants to wipe every person of color off the planet or destroy the galaxy or remove one person in every two from the galaxy for his own peace and quiet. On the other hand this sort of character will work very well as the . . .

The Boxing Glove Card

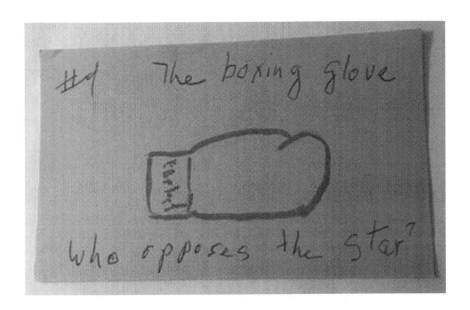

The Boxing Glove Card asks the question, "Who will oppose the star of the story?"

Card # 4, the boxing glove, asks the question, "Who will oppose the protagonist as she attempts to reach the goal?" That is, who's the antagonist of your novel? And why does the antagonist oppose the protagonist? In other words, who's the bad guy or gal? And why?

(Actually, it's more fun for you and your eventual reader if the antagonist has some redeeming virtues or at least is interesting.)

You can call him the villain if you like although your

antagonist might have a perfectly logical reason for his despicable actions, or at least they make sense to him. For example, in *January Jinx*, the first novel in my Calendar Mystery series, the ignorant, so-called sheriff of Campbell, Kansas, messes with the protagonist's goal of finding a job because he thinks he can extort a bunch of money from her.

It's not uncommon for a novice novelist to let the antagonist drive the plot car from the start and just keep on doing that until the plot car runs right off the road. The protagonist and the antagonist should be worthy of each other. And often the antagonist seems to be winning at the start of the novel. But sooner or later she probably should get her come-uppance.

Personally, I don't read lots of horror fiction, but I have read Stephen King's *Misery*. It has a superb yet terrifying antagonist, Annie Wilkes, who proclaims herself to be novelist Paul Sheldon's "number one fan." She is a really scary woman, that's for sure, and she does many bad things to the author, including forcing him to write another sappy novel in his sappy series. But eventually Paul wins out though he's left physically and mentally scarred.

Note: The antagonist doesn't have to be human. It can be a force of nature like the ocean in Ernest Hemingway's *The Old Man and the Sea*.

Card # 5

The Ear Card

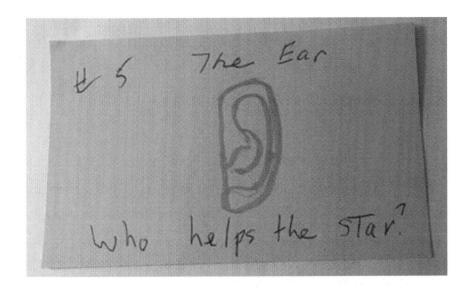

The Ear Card asks the question, "Who helps the star?"

This is one of my favorites. Your protagonist needs an ally, that is, someone to talk to, aka a confidant–for a very practical reason. What's that? you ask. Answer: so you can have dialogue. Fiction needs dialogue, that is, people talking, for it to come alive and jump up off the page. Also, with dialogue comes the ability to have conflict, the essence of what fiction is about.

I once had a student who didn't like to write dialogue, so she arranged for the protagonist of her science fiction novel not to understand a word of what other characters, members of an alien race, said. Gosh, that novel was dead in the water, and after a while I refused to read any more of it.

But I've gotten **way** ahead of myself. Suffice it to say you need to give the star of your novel someone to help him or her. At the very least, the ally can help the protagonist achieve the goals of the book by listening to the main character, that is, by serving as the protagonist's confidant.

You can have lots of fun with the ally since there are so many possibilities for this character besides providing someone to talk to. The ally can serve as the foil to the protagonist, for instance, the lippy girlfriend who's temperamentally very different from the serious female protagonist. The ally can be the comic relief sidekick. You can even let the ally oppose the protagonist sometimes by putting her down or by expressing doubts about his ability to make a million bucks.

Think about how interesting *The Silence of the Lambs* became when Thomas Harris made the loathsome cannibal Hannibal Lecter Clarice Starling's ally by giving her information that ultimately helped her find the killer.

The Match Card

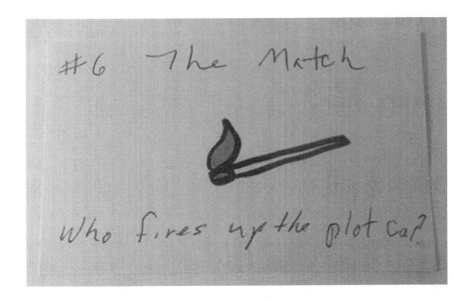

The Match Card asks the question,
"Who fires up the plot car?"

I know. I know. This is a bit of a mixed metaphor because you wouldn't really want to fire up a car. Still, I think the image of the match works well to get at the nature of another essential character that you'll need–someone who appears near the start of your novel to get the plot going. Once you're onto this sort of character, you'll see lots of them in the novels you read.

For example, a noir mystery novel often starts with some blonde, wearing a tight black suit and stilettos, swaying into the tough private eye's office to hire him to find out who murdered the victim or where her sister has gone. Several of Robert B. Parker's Spenser novels start with potential clients–though not usually sexy blondes–entering his office.

Sue Grafton has a woman wrongfully imprisoned for murdering her husband come to Kinsey Millhone to discover the true killer at the start of *A Is for Alibi*.

Early in Sara Paretsky's *Indemnity Only*, the first V. I. Warshawski mystery, the private investigator heads to her office at night through steamy Chicago to meet a potential client who refused to give his name to her answering service. But she needs to pay her bills, so she goes to her office, and thus she meets a man who wants her to find his son's missing girlfriend.

I've given examples from mystery fiction, but that's not to say writers of other sorts of fiction don't have this sort of character, too. For instance, J. R. R. Tolkien's *The Hobbit* begins with the wizard Gandalf arriving in town and carrying Bilbo Baggins off on an adventure.

Fiver's horrid dream of death and destruction to the warren sets in motion the long, epic journey of the rabbits in Richard Adams' *Watership Down*.

Wanting husbands for her daughters, Mrs. Bennet gets the plot of *Pride and Prejudice* going by sending her husband to call on the eligible and rich bachelor Mr. Bingley who has rented an estate nearby.

The Mouth Card

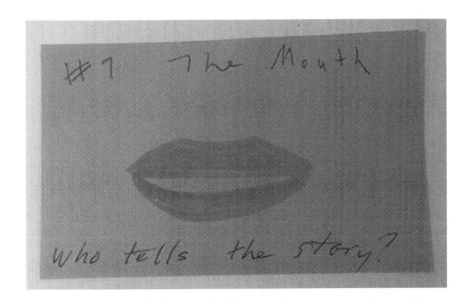

The Mouth Card asks the question,
"Who tells the story?"

Novelists have many options for narrators for their books and exactly how those narrators will present the narratives. I'll give you some common choices. I'll also note that sometimes, once you get into your novel, you might change your mind from what you write down on your card initially and what you later decide might be a better choice. The common terms for these choices are *viewpoint, point of view* or *perspective*.

By far the most common choice of point of view is

first person from the perspective of the protagonist, that is, the guy or gal in the driver's seat of the plot car. "That day when I saw this dame come in my office door, I said to myself, 'Mike Hammer, you know she's trouble. Gorgeous, but trouble.'"

But sometimes the first person narrator who tells the story in his own voice isn't the protagonist, but the second most important character in the work, the ally. This can be due to a very practical reason: the protagonist dies before the end of the novel. That's one reason why Chief Broom tells McMurphy's story in Ken Kesey's *One Flew Over the Cuckoo's Nest.* That's why Nick Carraway tells Gatsby's story and Ishmael tells Captain Ahab's. "And I alone remain to tell the tale . . ."

(Believe me when I tell you that few things annoy a reader more than getting to the end of a novel and finding out the person telling the story has been dead the whole time.)

Narrators can be innocent and say more than they understand, at least in the early pages of the novel, like Maisie in Henry James' *What Maisie Knew,* for example. Ishmael of *Moby Dick* is sort of an innocent, too.

A narrator can be reliable like Nick Carraway. Or a narrator can be unreliable, like drunken, deceitful Rachel Watson, *The Girl on the Train*, in Paula Hawkins' best-selling psychological thriller.

Speaking of that book, it's told in first person from

three women's points of view: Rachel, Anna and Megan. If you're an experienced novelist and want to use multiple first person viewpoint, I say go for it. If this will be your first novel, I'd say save this choice until your later books and keep this one simple.

Another very common choice is third person narration limited to the perspective of the protagonist. All of *January Jinx*, my first Calendar Mystery, and most of the second, *Fatal February,* stick to my protagonist's point of view in third person. One advantage of this sort of viewpoint is that it gives some distance for the reader on the action. It can do the same for you the novelist, too.

You might consider using an omniscient viewpoint, a popular choice in 19th century novels. That's when the narrator is some sort of godlike, all-knowing creature who looks down at the characters in the book. An early and famous example of this sort of point of view is Thackeray's *Vanity Fair* in which the narrator sometimes says things like "So what do you think of Becky Sharp now, dear reader?" Occasionally omniscient viewpoint cropped up in twentieth-century novels and even twenty-first century novels like Markus Zusak's *The Book Thief.*

But these days, most novelists stick to a third person perspective that's limited to a couple of characters, the young woman and her potential lover in a categorical romance, for instance, or no more than four or five even in a huge book like Stephen King's 800+ page American epic *The Stand.*

A word of caution about shifting from first to third person . . . In *T Is for Trespass*, Sue Grafton shifted back and forth from the third person viewpoint of the antagonist and the first person perspective of series protagonist Kinsey Millhone instead of sticking to Kinsey's perspective as Grafton did with most of the books in the series. But Grafton had lots of writing practice by then. She also started the book by using third person point of view to set up that expectation before she moved to Kinsey's usual first person viewpoint instead of springing that character's angle on the story suddenly and without warning later on.

Andy Weir used the device of Mark Watney's log to alternate smoothly between first person and third person sections of *The Martian*. Throughout *Mischief in March*, the third novel in my Calendar Mystery series, I have Minty Wilcox write in the journal that she calls *A. M. Wilcox's Investigation into All Things Daniel Price* and thus she moves back and forth between first person and third.

Summing Up About Characters

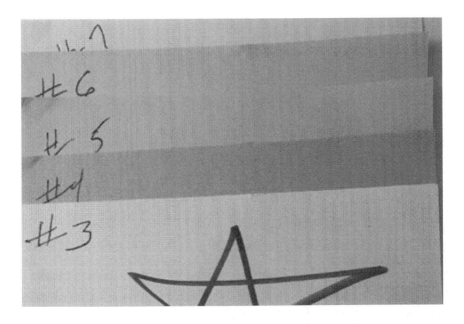

You've probably noticed that so far we've mostly talked about the characters, the people of the book you'll write. And maybe you've already noticed that your characters are fueling ideas for your novel. But before we move on to issues of plot, that is, driving the plot car to the end point of your journey or walking the plot tight rope, I'd like to point out a few more things about characters.

I'm a fan of mystery fiction, and mostly that's what I read with a smattering of science fiction, fantasy and historical fiction from time to time. So the first point about characters relates to mysteries in particular, but really you can do this with the principal characters of any novel.

1) Everybody has a secret.

2) A character can play two roles at once. This happens very often when the narrator tells his own story in first person. Or the ally is the narrator as in *The Great Gatsby*. But it can happen in other ways as well. Perhaps the ally also serves to start the plot by coming to the protagonist for help.

3) Any character can play a different role from the one she started out as. For instance, in mysteries, the protagonist/narrator can turn out to be the killer. An apparent antagonist/suspect can turn out to be an ally. An ally, that is, the confidant or sidekick, can turn out to be the killer. The character that gets the plot rolling can turn out to be the killer. (I just love it when a skillful writer fools me. Don't you?)

4) Sometimes you need more than one of any type of character. In a novel, quite a few characters can pose a threat to the protagonist accomplishing her goal. In Sara Paretsky's *Indemnity Only*, for instance, a crime boss sends a couple of his goons to pick up Vic, the tough female private eye. In my own *January Jinx*, the first novel in my Calendar Mystery series, the protagonist, Minty Wilcox wants to find a suitable job in old Kansas City. But not only does the major antagonist interfere with her reaching her goal, but so does Minty's mother who views her daughter's wish to help with household finances as a sign of her own failure to manage them.

5) If you have trouble finding directions for where your plot car could go, ask your characters. They might surprise you with their inventive suggestions. Sometimes a character might suggest something outrageous. For instance, when I was drafting my second novel, set in a dystopian future, the antagonist wanted to kill the protagonist very early, but I couldn't let that happen of course. But the antagonist's attempts to kill the protagonist made for some really dandy plot developments.

Now, before we get to the plot cards.

The Place Card

The Place Card asks the questions,
"Where and when does the novel take place?"

One of the elements I've always loved about reading novels is their ability to transport me to faraway places and long ago times like the Ancient World of the Marcus Didius Falco mysteries by Lindsey Davis or the medieval world of Brother Cadfael in the historical mysteries of Ellis Peters. There's a whole romance subgenre that takes place in Britain during the Regency period. James Church's fascinating Inspector O series takes place in modern-day North Korea. The sky isn't even the limit.

Consider Andy Weir's *The Martian* that takes place, at least in part, on Mars. *Artemis*, Weir's second book, takes place in a city on the moon.

The times and the locales for your novel will heavily shape its content because setting supplies many things. Growing up in a small town, suburbia, or a big city all will affect the nature of your protagonist, for instance, in different ways.

It very well might supply be the antagonist like the frigid cold of a Siberian winter in Alexander Solzhenitsyn's *One Day in the Life of Ivan Denisovich*.

Weather can matter a lot in fiction, in part for the mood of the piece. (If you place characters on a space ship headed to Mars, you might not have weather, but you might have debris hitting the ship.)

Setting will supply minor characters. For example, the doorman who greets your protagonist when he comes home from a long day on Wall Street will have no place in the small riverside town you've chosen for where your protagonist grows up in the 1950's. For that book you might need an old lady who runs the corner grocery store instead.

Something else that will affect how your book turns out is when it takes place: past, present or future, and what each choice requires. Specifically if you choose some past time as I did for my Calendar Mysteries set in Kansas City around 1900, you might need to do research. Setting your book in an imagined future as did Andy Weir for *The Martian* and *Artemis* might require research as well. Using the present day, as I'm considering for the contemporary cozy mystery series I haven't started yet, might seem like a safe choice, but it very well might require research into police work.

Another thing you will have to take into account is the amount of time involved in the action of your novel. Consider the difference between *One Day in the Life of Ivan Denisovich,* a very short novel, and Leo Tolstoy's *War and Peace* and *Anna Karina*, both very long novels that span years.

And not at all inconsequently, setting can provide obstacles to your protagonist in achieving his or her goal.

This brings us to . . .

Card # 9

The Wall Card

**The Wall Card asks the question,
"What could possibly go wrong?"**

In truth, Card # 9 is a placeholder because you will need lots more than just one wall or obstacle that keeps your protagonist from achieving her goal right away. This card is one of my favorite cards because I have so much fun brainstorming all the things that could possibly go wrong in my hero's journey.

Exactly how many hurdles you need your hero to vault is partly a matter of scale. Hemingway needed lots more obstacles for Jake to surmount in the full-length novel *The*

Sun Also Rises than he needed for Santiago in the novella *The Old Man in the Sea.*

Once, Janice Young Brooks, author of the historical novel *Guests of the Emperor* and as Jill Churchill the Jane Jeffries mystery series, confided in me that she likes to have "thirty-six things" to put in a book before she starts. They might not all be obstacles, but still she knows what she's aiming for.

A more answerable question is where you can look for the obstacles you might place in front of your protagonist.

1) A physical impairment can provide obstacles to a protagonist. For example, the protagonist of the Cormoran Strike series by Robert Galbraith (aka J.K. Rowling) lost part of a leg in Afghanistan and often this physical impairment interferes with his life and his investigations.

2) Another source for obstacles preventing your protagonist from reaching his final goal right away might come in the form of some inner conflict. Self-doubt, shyness, lack of confidence, any of those would be good.

3) Other characters in the novel can provide obstacles. The major antagonist is an obvious choice, but the other characters can as well.

(These characters don't necessarily have to be alive. In the Inspector Ian Rutledge series, set just after World War 1, by the mother-son writing team of Charles Todd, Hamish MacLeod, a soldier that Rutledge ordered executed, speaks up from the back seat and sows doubt in

Rutledge's mind almost every time Rutledge drives a car.)

4) The settings can provide powerful physical obstacles to the protagonist getting where he needs to be. Again think about the bitter cold of *One Day in the Life of Ivan Denisovich.*

And now another transition . . .

A Brief History of Plot

Way back in 4th Century BCE, the Greek philosopher Aristotle gave the first guidelines to plot structure when he said that a tragedy needs three parts: beginning, middle, and end, later called Act 1, Act 2, and Act 3. He also stated that the beginning isn't necessarily preceded by any significant action, the middle grows out of the beginning, and the end grows out of middle. A successful plot might contain a surprise like some sort of shift in the action or finding out a secret from the past.

This very simple statement belies all the variations, refinements, arguments and applications to assorted kinds of storytelling that have developed since that time. Those variations included that of Horace, a Roman poet, who later said that a play needed five acts. Both Aristotle and Horace were talking about stories performed on a stage with live actions. Some differences and divergences of how plots were structured came about with the novel.

One of the earliest ways extended fiction was structured was the still popular picaresque plot, so named because Miguel de Cervantes used this type of plot in *Don Quixote,* first published in 1606, in which the hero and his sidekick, a rascal or *picaro* named Sancho Panza, go on one adventure after another.

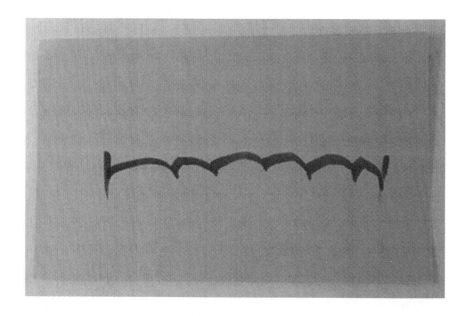

The picaresque plot tends to have a bunch of episodes loosely strung together, that is, just one darned thing after another. You might recognize it from the very popular *Fifty Shades of Grey.* (Honestly, I haven't read that novel.

But a friend of mine read the first few chapters and reported that the book seemed episodic to her.)

Charles Dickens structured *The Pickwick Papers*, first published in installments in 1836, in similar fashion though he did frame the adventures with an overall story about Pickwick's wedding proposal to a woman who sued him for breach of promise for not following through at the end of the novel.

I'll omit some of the other variations of plot structure and skip to Syd Field's *Screenplay: The Foundations of Screenwriting*, first published in 1979.

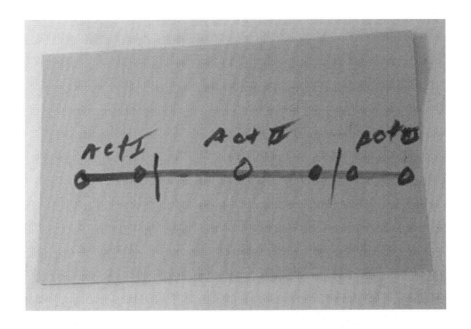

Field said that successful movies tend to have three parts: Act 1 that runs for about thirty minutes (about thirty script pages), Act 2 that runs sixty minutes (about sixty pages), and Act 3, that runs to no more than thirty minutes. Field also says that a successful movie has six essential scenes.

Not long after that, Robert J. Ray in *The Weekend Novelist* described the structure of a novel as similar to Field's paradigm, but with more pages in each act because the novelist must put much more on the page than the screenwriter does. Suffice it to say that the plot of a novel needs several scenes, six or even as many as nine including scenes that cut up the large Act 2 into manageable parts.

Scriptwriters are often so precise about bringing in the essential scenes that you can time them. "Hey, hey, wait for it. Wait for it. Ah, here comes Plot Point 1, right on schedule at minute 29." Novelists generally aren't so precise about hitting the plot points, but still successful novels usually place these important scenes at fairly regular intervals.

W. Somerset Maugham, author of almost twenty novels, once famously said, "There are three rules for writing a novel. Unfortunately, no one knows what they are." That hasn't kept other writers from writing books on the subject and coming up with more rules, up to ten in one instance. My own take on this is that the novel you write tells you what it needs and wants to be as you write it, including decisions on structure. For example, although the classical template might dictate otherwise, Suzanne Collins divided *The Hunger Games* into three parts, all about the same length: Part I–138 pages, Part II–106 pages, Part III–130 pages.

As for myself, a writer primarily of mystery fiction, I prefer a more logical plot than the picaresque novel has, not one darned thing after another, but a tightly connected chain of events: that is, one more thing happens because of what happened before and the whole situation getting more and more complicated until things come together in a big scene in which the whole situation gets resolved.

My favorite representation of plot is the inverted check mark with the three major acts and the six major scenes overlaid on it because this diagram shows how the action and the tension of a well plotted novel build to the highest point of intensity in the book that's resolved before its end.

Instead of thinking of plot structure as a formula, think of it as a skeleton, the bare bones on which you need to build your novel.

Next, we'll move on to Card # 10, the first of your six scene cards. But before we do, here's an important question for you: Where will you get the ideas for these scenes? Why from your obstacle cards, of course. At this point, you might not have enough ideas for all six scenes, so you might need to leave some of your scene cards blank.

Card # 10
The First Scene Card
(aka the Hook)

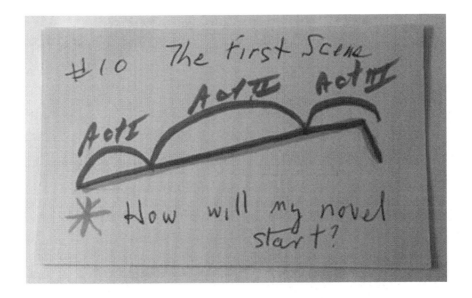

The First Scene Card asks the question,
"How will my novel start?"

Entire books have been written on the importance of the start of your novel. I won't list any of these books here. But I will say that, above all else, the first scene of a novel must be compelling. It needs to pull your reader into your story, so it's often called a hook. It also usually introduces the protagonist. Your protagonist, what she wants, her world, just what sort of a person she is, and something of her backstory are the basic subjects for Act 1 of your novel. That's a lot for you to figure out before you decide where your book starts.

You probably won't want to start with your protagonist's birth, Dickens' masterfully written *David Copperfield* to the contrary.

Bernard Cornwell begins *The Last Kingdom*, the first book in his epic Warrior Chronicle series, by telling us that the book (and series) protagonist Uhtred wants back his ancestral lands stolen from him. And then at the bottom of page one, we move right into Uhtred's account of the day in 866 when his life changed, that is, when he first saw the Danes invading England.

Many beginning writers start with the protagonist waking up in the morning and then take him through the ordinary routine of shower, sh*t and shave. (Actually, I'm quoting from a student's story.) Believe me. This has been done before, and it hardly ever works. Really you want to start your novel on a day when something different happens.

Now, I realize that the opening to your book might be very vague to you or even absolutely wrong when you first make out this card. In his memoirs *Seldom Disappointed* Tony Hillerman talks about the drawer he had full of first chapters, that is, false starts to some of his Jim Chee and Joe Leaphorn mysteries. (Wonderful series, one of my all time favorites.)

So for now at least, think of a day in the life of your

protagonist when something out of the routine happens or recently happened or that protagonist finds out about. It's not a business-as-usual moment. It's the start of something different. Uhtred's life changes completely when the Vikings arrive in his world.

Think about the start of *Harry Potter and the Sorcerer's Stone*, on what was decidedly not an ordinary day. Mr. Dursley sees a cat reading a map and several men wearing brightly colored cloaks. Owls are sighted flying in daylight all over the country. What is going on? Dursley wonders, and so do Rowling's readers.

Often it's when your *match* character appears. In walks this dame of noir mystery fiction, for instance. The wizard Gandalf arrives in the little Hobbit town to fetch Bilbo Baggins off on an adventure.

Some novels start *in medias res*, that is, in the middle of things. A crime novel might start with the discovery of the body, for instance, another extraordinary event even for cops.

Now let's travel in our minds to the very end of your narrative and make a card for the last scene of your novel.

The Last Scene

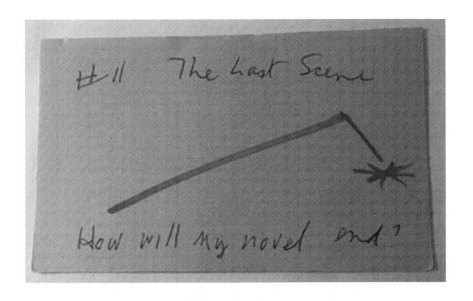

**The Last Scene Card asks the question,
"How will my novel end?"**

By now, you shouldn't be too surprised that the second scene card you complete gives the answer to the question on the Heart Card for your novel, the answer that you put on the back of your Outcome Card. But here, you can expand on it a bit to include the following options.

Yes, and furthermore . . .

Yes, but . . .

No, and furthermore . . .

No, but . . .

Yes, Cinderella gets her Prince Charming, and **furthermore** they live happily ever after.

No, Gatsby doesn't get Daisy and **furthermore** he's murdered. **But** Nick considers him worth more than a whole lot of other people including Daisy Buchanan that Gatsby tried so hard to woo and win.

Because I don't like to use spoilers when I'm writing about the novels you might read, I'll make some of my examples for the last scene fairly generic.

In Westerns, the hero, having vanquished the villain in a shoot-out and leaving the girl behind, rides off into the sunset.

In categorical romance novels, the girl and boy might ride off together in the sunset on the same horse.

In epic fantasy, the dragon slain and the treasure retrieved, the hero and his buddies celebrate in a victory feast.

Nick Carraway packs his bags, sells his car, prepares to go back home to the Midwest on the train, and reflects upon the lesson he learned from Gatsby.

In the last scene of *One Day in the Life of Ivan Denisovich*, the protagonist decides that he's had a fairly decent day, almost a happy one, one of the 3,653 days in his ten-year stretch in the prison camp, the three extra days being for leap years.

January Jinx, the first book in my Calendar Mystery series, has a **yes, but** ending. The novel starts with Minty

Wilcox on her way to seek employment as a "business girl," that is, a typist/stenographer, in Kansas City, a place that could downright deadly in 1899. Does she get that job? Okay, I'll reveal that yes she does. (And furthermore, she meets this really good-looking gent.) But . . . That's all you get.

Traditionally called the *dénouement* or unraveling or untying or the clearing up of your plot, the last scene of your book presents the aftermath of the next scene we'll work on. The last scene ties up any remaining loose ends in the plot, and as is sometimes the case in series fiction, possibly sets up the next book. Do note that sometimes readers complain bitterly about a cliffhanger at the end of a novel, even if you've tied up the main plot, but especially if you don't, so really I can't advise it.

The Climax Scene

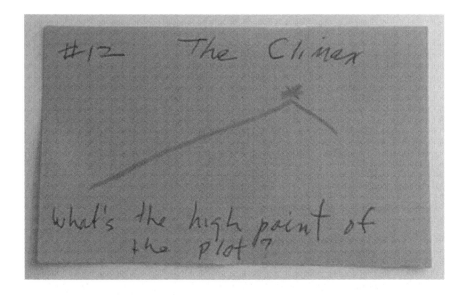

The Climax Scene Card asks the question, "What's the high point of my novel's plot?"

Called the climax, the crisis, or the catastrophe, this scene is the moment of the highest intensity of your plot, the part of your plot that the entire book has led up to. The climax scene can and often does show the do-or-die moment. It's the highest point on the inverted check mark. Perhaps it involves the final confrontation between the protagonist and antagonist. Christopher Vogler in *The Writer's Journey*, his excellent book on mythic structure for fiction and scriptwriters, calls this scene "the ultimate ordeal." In a coming-of-age novel or a novel of ideas, the strongest, most powerful and intense scene may be when the protagonist has an epiphany about himself or life itself.

Traditionally, the climactic scene brings about a change of the protagonist's fate, for better–he gets the girl and lives happily ever after with her–or for worse–he dies.

It's the point in the novel when the protagonist finally resolves the problem of the book or dies trying, when Captain Ahab, for instance, finally confronts the whale in *Moby Dick* and dies.

In a western, it might be the shoot-out between the sheriff and the leader of the robber gang. In a traditional British murder mystery, it's the scene in the library when the detective reveals the identity of the killer. In a romance, the lovers resolve their differences at last. In a coming-of-age novel, it might be the scene in which the protagonist finally discovers the truth about his father or her mother. In Stephen King's psychological horror thriller *Misery*, Paul Sheldon finally vanquishes his number one fan, the cruel nurse Annie Wilkes.

Sometimes the climax might be a fairly intimate scene, with just the villain and the hero duking it out in the dark. Many mysteries have this sort of pivotal scene, but some novels have much larger climactic scenes with whole armies facing each other on the battlefield. I've grown to admire the climactic scenes in the cozy mysteries of Nancy Martin and the romantic adventures of Janet Evanovich for the way both authors bring together every major character in a dramatic, yet comic scene that resolves the mystery at last.

An important tip: avoid letting another character rescue the protagonist at the climax, a fairly common mistake for beginners. In a good, solid plot, the protagonist's lover can't come riding up on a white horse, fell the villain, and cut the ropes that tie the damsel to the railroad track. If the damsel is the protagonist, she has to do all of that herself and have the villain's neck under her dainty foot when the lover rides up on his white horse, slightly too late.

So at least tentatively figure out which of the obstacles the hero confronts is the most intense, the do-or-die moment for your book to describe briefly on your Climax Scene Card.

Card # 13
The Midpoint Scene

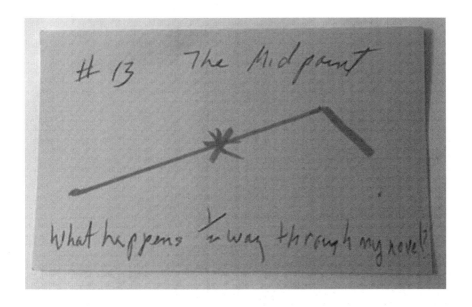

The Midpoint Scene Card asks the question, "What happens halfway through my novel?"

About midway through your novel, you will need a scene in which the plot takes a surprising turn of events or shifts in a new direction. The midpoint scene is very important structurally for your novel. For one thing, if you have a strong midpoint scene, your novel will not sag in the middle, a flaw I've heard at least one successfully published novelist complain about.

The midpoint scene is sometimes called the rug pulling because things seem to have been going well for the protagonist, but now something happens that changes everything for him, so he might have to start over again or almost. (The middle point of a *W* is a really good way of representing this part of a novel.)

For example, after a great struggle involving many challenges, the lone mountain climber grabs a loose rock and falls into a crevasse and breaks her leg. Oh gosh, the reader says. Will she get out of there? And how? Will she make it to the top? (FYI: she can't get rescued here either.)

In her Adam Dalgliesh novel *Original Sin*, P. D. James waits until midpoint for the murder to occur after we've gotten to know all the characters including the detectives, the suspects and the victim.

In a romance, the guy and the gal get to know each other or at least try to in the first part of Act 2, but about halfway through Act 2 they have a misunderstanding or a falling out. For example, around the middle of *Pride and Prejudice,* Mr. Darcy proposes to Elizabeth Bennet for all the wrong reasons and quite rightly she refuses him.

The midpoint doesn't necessarily have to be negative. Perhaps in the first half of the book, your heroine has overcome some of her initial obstacles to achieving her goal of getting the guy. And now, strengthened by surmounting earlier obstacles, she's gained the ability to confront the more challenging obstacles to come in the second half of the novel.

In her excellent book *How to Write Killer Fiction,*

Carolyn Wheat says that in the first half of Act 2 of a mystery we have the first detection. In this section typically the detective is on the false track or the bumbling police detective gets it all wrong. But at midpoint something happens that leads to the second detection and the correct solution. The detective's prime suspect turns up dead, for instance. Or Miss Marple takes over the investigation.

In *The Hunger Games*, Katniss Everdeen receives her first gift from her sponsor on page 188 of the 374-page novel.

Once you've figured out your midpoint scene, you'll need two more scenes, both that set up major plot points.

The First Set-Up Scene

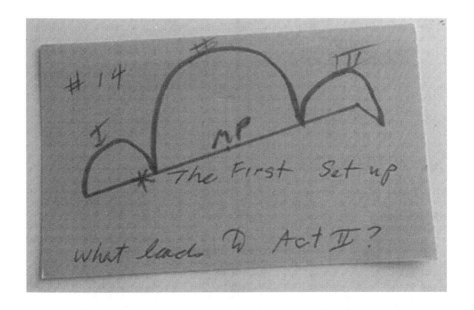

The First Set-Up Card asks the question, "What leads to Act 2 of my novel?"

Near the end of Act 1 of your novel, after you've hooked your reader with the beginning scene and shown your protagonist and her world, you need a scene in which the protagonist commits to the action required in the book. Syd Field called it Plot Point 1 of a movie script and other authors have used the same term for the novel. But I prefer the term *set-up* since that's what this scene does. Specifically, the first set-up scene sets up the action that follows in Act 2 in which the heroine confronts the problem and tries to resolve the situation by jumping the hurdles in her way.

It's like the moment in a boxing match–after the fighter you favor has strutted into the ring, likewise his opponent–when the bell rings and one of boxers throws the first punch, thus setting the tone and character of the match. Or the tennis player puts the ball into play.

The private eye might have signed the contract earlier, but now he emotionally commits to it.

In a romance, the heroine and her love interest, having met cute in Act 1, decide to try to make a go of it somehow.

In fantasy, the first set up happens when the hero accepts the call to adventure and sets off on his epic adventure through Middle Earth or goes off to Hogwarts for his first year of wizardry school.

In Theresa Hupp's historical Western novels *Lead Me Home* and *Forever Mine,* the characters begin their journey on the Oregon Trail in the first set-up scene.

The Second Set-Up Scene

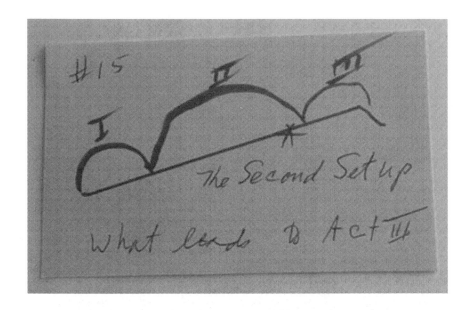

**The Second Set-up Scene Card asks the question,
"How leads to Act 3 of my novel?"**

Similar to the first set-up scene, the second set-up scene, more commonly called Plot Point 2, sets up Act 3 of the novel. That is, it sets up the climactic scene of the novel, the most intense scene of the novel, and also the aftermath of the climax, the dénouement. In the second set-up scene, for example, the hero prepares to make one more attempt to defeat the villain, or the antagonist throws one last, truly daunting challenge in the hero's way. The protagonist girds her loins, or the villain musters his troops.

In Western fiction, the sheriff sets off to meet the swaggering bad guys in the middle of the street of the little cow town.

In romantic fiction, the hero prepares one last attempt to woo and win the gal he loves.

One of my all time favorite second set-up scenes in crime fiction appears in Dick Francis's debut novel, *Odds Against*. Sid Halley, already handicapped with a missing hand, wakes up strapped to a boiler about to explode. Oh boy, you say to yourself, Will Sid get out of there in time to avoid dying? How will he do it? If he gets free, does he go after the bad guy and catch him? No spoilers from me. You have to read this great novel for yourself to find out.

Don't worry if you don't have much of an idea for this scene when you initially make out your cards. It will come. Now let's move on to one more plot card.

The Subplot Card

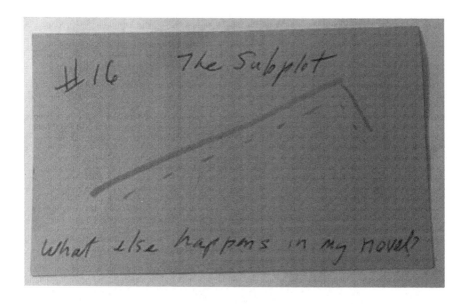

**The subplot card asks the question,
"What else happens in my novel?"**

The novel is a huge beast and needs a lot of plot to reach the minimum required 40,000 words that will go into it. One way a writer often finds those words is with subplots. (Please note that the subplot card, like the wall card, might be a placeholder.)

Indeed, though the publishing industry is always changing, it's still fairly common advice in publishing that if an author wants a career, she will write a series or trilogy on the theory that the more you write the more you sell.

And while the reader expects the major "who wants what?" plot to be resolved in each novel, the subplots and the continuing characters in the series often serve to pull the reader from one novel to the next.

Exactly what the subplot contains depends in part on the genre of the novel. For example, in romantic suspense, the love relationship provides the main plot line and the mystery/suspense provides the subplot with lots of fun interferences with the main plot in play. If you're writing a mystery novel, you'll flip that with the mystery plot primary and a romantic subplot secondary.

Many writers, no matter the genre of the novel, might introduce the protagonist's family and/or friends into the novels to pull the readers from book to book. Will Stephanie Plum favor Ranger or Morelli this time? the fans of Janet Evanovich's very popular and long-lasting series wonder. They also wonder about the goings-on of Stephanie's family, especially the outrageous Grandma Mazur.

Each novel in my Calendar Mystery series has its own murder mystery, resolved by the end of the book. But each might also have two or three subplots that carry over from book to book: Minty Wilcox's goal of getting a suitable job for a woman in Kansas City around 1900, the romantic subplot with Daniel Price, and Minty's on-going relationships with her family members. Also, *Fatal February*, the second novel in the series, has an additional mystery subplot besides the major plot line. *Mischief in March*, the third novel, has a romantic subplot that features two long time supporting characters in the series.

If you look closely at the picture of Card #16, you'll notice that the subplot has its own plot line. Very typically, the subplot begins after the major plot is in place. The subplot might end pretty much before the second set-up scene, or it might end in the dénouement. Some authors put a cliffhanger related to a subplot on the last page of one novel to hook the readers into anticipating the next one. For example, I put a cliffhanger at the end of *Mischief in March* setting up a new mystery plot that I later resolved in a short story.

I'd be wary of doing that however. Some readers deeply resent that sort of ending. And it also put me in a bit of a pickle of how to resolve the issue for my readers in a timely manner. Ultimately, I wrote and published the short story called "Detectives' Honeymoon," later included in *Old Time Stories*, Book 4 of my Calendar Mystery series.

And now let's move on to Card # 17.

The Genre Card

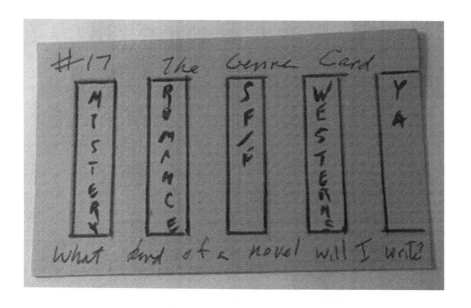

The Genre Card asks the question, "What kind of a novel will I write?"

Ordinarily, I don't ascribe to the saying, "Write what you know" because when writers don't know something they need to put in their books, they do research. But in this case, I advise that you write what you know. That is, you should write the kind of novel you're most familiar with because you read novels in that genre all the time.

To narrow this down a little bit, let's imagine you're at the library and you're looking for something tasty to read. Where do you go? To the children's department even though you're an adult? Science Fiction/Fantasy/Horror? Mysteries? Romance? Westerns? General Fiction that might include literary and historical novels? You should probably write whatever type of novel you check out and bring home from the library. (You can perform a similar exercise by figuring out which genre you gravitate to in a bookstore or on Amazon and Barnes & Noble.)

To narrow the subject of the genre down even more, by the time you get to Card # 17, you've made quite a few decisions that affect the kind of book you're writing, for instance, the gender and age of your protagonist. Consider the differences between Tucker MacBean, a boy just entering the Seventh Grade in present-day Kansas in Lisa Harkrader's children's novel *Cool Beans: The Further Adventures of Beanboy*, and grown-up Lady Edith aka Edie Gilchrist in Eloisa James' take on the Rapunzel story in her fairy tale romance *Once Upon a Tower* set in London in 1824.

What sorts of plot developments you include will also affect what kind of book you end up writing. Noir mystery fiction has loads more blood and guts, not to mention foul language and a cynical view of life, than your typical cozy.

But why does genre matter anyway?

Well, I assume that you might like a return on the time and effort it took you to write your novel by having people buy it, read it, and even review it once you've finished it. The chances of that happening increase if your novel fits in a niche, the smaller the better, so you won't compete against authors like James Patterson in the Mystery, Thriller, and Suspense category of fiction, for example.

These days big genres like fantasy, mysteries, women's fiction in general, and romance more specifically have developed many, very specific subgenres. For example, the cozy mystery subgenre can be further subdivided into culinary mysteries, cozy mysteries that include hobbies and crafts of all kinds, and cozy mysteries that have animals. There are even subcategories for Christian cozy mysteries and cozy mysteries with magic like the novels and stories in my Cinderella, P. I. fairy tale mysteries for grown-ups.

Jim Butcher practically invented a new subgenre–urban fantasy–with his Harry Dresden series described by a reviewer as "magic and wizardry meet hard-boiled detective fiction."

Books like Butcher's *Storm Front* bring us to a bit of an issue. For years, the standard advice in publishing was to avoid crossovers or mashups for fear of confusing potential readers, but that didn't seem to deter Butcher who has published fifteen novels as well as three story collections in the Dresden Files series. The popularity of Diana Gabaldon's *Outlander* and its sequels seems not to be affected by their mix of time travel, adventure, and Scottish historical romance.

We'll explore the issue of genre a little more with the discussion of Card # 18.

Card # 18
The Reader Card

The Reader Card asks the question,
"Who will read my novel?"

By now, you probably have a fairly good idea of who will
want to read your novel. For one thing, chances are good
that your target or ideal reader reads the same sorts of
novels as you do, and lots of them, too.

Try to get specific in identifying your ideal reader. For
instance, if she reads women's fiction, does she prefer
cozy mysteries with women sleuths? Are the sleuths
amateurs or police officers? Or does your ideal reader love
romance novels? Must those books be wholesome and

clean, with maybe a shy kiss at the end? Or does your reader relish erotica with lots of heavy breathing?

Is your ideal reader a male who enjoys a blood and guts, action-packed thriller with some very specific sex scenes?

As like as not, your ideal reader is the same gender as your protagonist and a similar age as well because it's customary in publishing that the reader is about the same age as the protagonist of a novel. (In Young Adult fiction, the protagonist might be a bit older than the reader in order to serve as a role model.)

Long ago I had the fantasy that someday I'd write the book that everybody reads the year it comes out. I haven't written that novel yet. But Suzanne Collins might have come close with *The Hunger Games*. A friend's twelve-year-old granddaughter read those books and so have I, many decades older. Some of my contemporaries have read every one of J.K. Rowling's Harry Potter books.

Speaking of that writer, Rowling has written and published four novels in the Cormoran Strike series so different from the Harry Potter series that she uses the pseudonym of Robert Galbraith. The target readers for those two series are very different and their expectations quite different as well.

While we're talking about the reader, let's move to Card # 19.

Card # 19
The Intention Card

The Intention Card asks the question, "How will my novel affect the reader?"

The novel is a tool of infinite possibilities, a sort of Swiss Army knife with a million blades. That's one of the reasons I read. When I pluck a novel off the new mysteries shelf at the library and bring it home, I'm filled with hope that this novel will surprise me. Maybe the author will say something new or at least in a different way: tease me, thrill me, move me to laughter and to tears in the same book, make me think about the human experience in some new way, expand my life, or simply help me escape my troubling or mundane world for a few hours.

At this point, I'll circle back to my brief history of plot by mentioning that Aristotle said the purpose of a tragedy is catharsis, to purge the audience with pity and fear by seeing a man fall from grace through his own hubris.

As for me, I believe that laughter is the best medicine for whatever ails you in life, so I like to make people laugh or at least smile when they read my novels and stories. And I give my stories happy endings.

So what's the primary intention of your novel? Do you want to entertain your reader by scaring the heck out of him with your horror fiction? Do you want to make her feel sexy with your erotic romance? Or do you want to create a puzzle in a cozy mystery for your reader to figure out? Maybe you want to move your reader to empathize with other people who have survived great adversity, to understand some truth or theme about the human condition from someone else's suffering that your reader can experience vicariously.

In addition, one of the most splendid things about the novel is its ability to say something worthwhile. So give at least a tentative answer to the question the Intention Card asks.

And now here's one last card.

Card # 20
The Cover Card

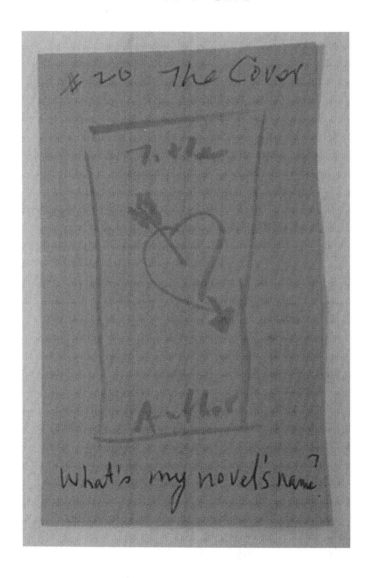

The Cover Card asks the question,
"What's my novel's name?"

The wise organizers of NaNoWriMo say that those who have covers for their projects before they start drafting them are 60% more likely to write it that those who don't. I think possibly that simply giving your novel a name helps make it real to you.

So on your last card at least give the tentative title for your novel, your name or the pseudonym you've always dreamed of using, and possibly an image for your cover.

You might also want to put " a blurb" on the flip side of your cover card. That is, in a very few words describe the novel you want to write. Here's an example: "an action-packed thriller with a wounded hero."

Good luck with making your personalized deck of cards and answering the questions they pose. Some of you might answer all of the questions as you make your cards. Some of you won't answer any. I suspect many of you will answer some of the questions, but will leave the backs of some of the cards blank to come back to later.

I recommend at this point that you answer the questions fast with at most only as much information as you can fit on the back of a 3" by 5" card. You probably will need more cards when you get to the obstacle cards, perhaps as many as Janice Young Brooks' thirty-six, but at least six, one for each of your scene cards.

Have a wonderful time and when you're done, come back, and I'll give you tips on what to do next.

PART 2: Draft Your Novel

Tips on Time Management

Tips on Drafting a Novel

Tips on Time Management

What's next? On the face of it, that's an easy question to answer. Once you've created your cards, answered all the questions on the cards, and devised a number of obstacle cards, you will write your novel. Right? Not so fast.

I think it really helps to gear up to the process of writing a novel because once you're working actively on your book it will consume lots of your time. Having some time management plans and solid work habits in place might ultimately save you time. So let's get cracking.

<> <> <>

As I prepared to retype "How to Write a Novel in Your Spare Time," the handout that I used in both credit and noncredit classes for a long time, I was rather startled to realize that I've been seriously going after a career as a novelist for more than thirty years. In that time, many things have changed about the publishing industry, but one element remains the same. It's not uncommon for novelists to write a novel in their spare time while they work a day job or even a couple to pay the bills.

Just the other day, I read an article in *The Kansas City Star* about L. L. McKinney whose first novel for young adults, *A Blade So Black*, recently came out from a major publisher. Like many writers, McKinney wrote in the evenings after she got off her day job and on weekends as well. When interviewed, she still worked that day job and looked forward to the time when she could write full time.

That's been an issue for authors going way back. For instance, P. D. James had her first mystery published in 1962 when she was forty-two, but she didn't retire from working full time until she was fifty-nine. During those seventeen years, she wrote about six more books, or one every three years. She once said that actually she got more writing done when she worked because people respected her writing time more.

Right now you might be saying to yourself that if James had written full time, she would have written more books. Maybe, but she was the breadwinner for her family and caring for a needy husband, so she had to work. Some creative people have partners or parents who support them. Lots of us don't, so we have no choice about whether or not we work.

Note: only about fourteen percent of writers make a living at it. These include nonfiction writers, so I suspect the overall percentage for novelists is lower.

We remember the success stories like Stephen King's first advance of $400,000 for *Carrie* or Jean Auel's $23 million deal for her series that started with *Clan of the Cave Bear*. It was like winning the lottery back then, and it rarely happens these days. Even back then, an author usually had to write more than one book before he might get the interest of an agent. Trained and working as a psychologist at the time, Jonathan Kellerman was writing his third Alex Delaware novel–in his garage–before he got someone interested in the first.

These days even a writer with a good project can't break through the wall of the gatekeepers outside traditional publishers. For example, *The Martian* was picked up only after Andy Weir self-published it on his website. Given that, if we want to get published, we'd all better start working part-time on that novel.

But having a day job isn't entirely bad. Being out and about in the workaday world gives us material and broader perspectives, besides social interaction. Overhearing a lively conversation at Starbucks between two women dressed in exercise togs might give you ideas for dialogue, for instance. The panhandler at the corner close to your office might give you an idea for a great character.

Now let's talk about time in earnest. It's a really critical factor for people who want to write novels in their spare time. You probably want to know how long it will take you to write a novel. That depends.

Since I first devised my "How to Write a Novel in Your Spare Time" handout, some clever people came up with NaNoWriMo, that is, National Novel Writing Month, when a bunch of crazy people like me attempt to write a 50,000-word novel in the thirty days of November. This effort started small, but in 2015 almost a half a million people all over the world attempted to meet the challenge. About 50,000 succeeded including me. I also participated in NaNoWriMo in 2014, 2017, and 2018.

All four of my NaNoWriMo projects so far seemed more like brainstorms with a few scenes interspersed here and there than real drafts, but NaNoWriMo works really well to punch through any writer's block you might have. Plus the organizers offer incentives and tons of advice from highly respected novelists. One year Jim Butcher of the very popular Harry Dresden urban fantasy series wrote a tongue-in-cheek piece about why you really wouldn't want to write a novel in a month.

But if you're working full time, you might not have the typical four hours a day free a retired person like me needs to crank out 1,667 words a day.

In his book *The Weekend Novelist*, Robert J. Ray presents a very clear program for working on a novel every weekend and taking it through three drafts in a year.

I don't offer as neat a package for writing a novel as Mr. Ray does in *The Weekend Novelist*. And in my experience, I've found that it's better to work on your novel everyday, at least a little bit, to keep up your momentum and thus avoid the guilt that comes from not working on it and the despair of having to gear up again to get going on your book.

Here are some specific tips for maximizing your time as you draft your novel.

1) Work on your novel everyday if only to brainstorm some aspect of it in your journal.

A piece of advice for beginning writers so common that no one knows exactly where it came from is you have to write a million words and throw them away before you can become a writer. Yeah, that makes me wince, too, and I think it's not true because books like my *Novel Basics* will help you get there faster.

Still, keeping a journal and writing in it every day is a painless way to get those million words down. Indeed, I can count on the fingers of one hand how many days I haven't made at least a weather note in my log or journal since I started journaling on January 1, 1985.

So I recommend you keep one and write in it daily. Practice creates writing fluency and speed. It provides a place to store and to work out ideas. And it helps you develop your own voice.

Here's a tip from Joel Goldman, international best-selling crime author. Download a dictation app to your smart phone, so when you get a bright idea about something to put in your novel while you're walking in your neighborhood or running on a stationary bike at the gym, you can speak it into your phone and the transcription of your note will await you online when you get home.

2) Learn to compose at a keyboard, so you can type your novel from the get-go.

My junior year in high school, I took Personal Typing. And I was constantly afraid that the big wheezing electric machine would eat my pinky fingers if I let them slide over the edge of the keyboard on either side.

But you know what? That typing class was the most worthwhile class I took in high school. Much later, when I went to graduate school to get my doctorate, I taught myself to compose at a keyboard by typing the journal I kept for my Romantic Poetry class.

I do have a very well published friend who writes her first drafts by hand or at least the start of them. But I see no merit or glory in it at all. It's faster to type the first draft and your novel will be much easier to revise later on, not to mention you'll be able to read what you wrote. (I'm notorious among my students for my bad handwriting, and it's only gotten worse as time has gone by due to arthritis in my hands.)

3) Devise a time management chart.

My freshman year in college, the professor in Orientation class had us draw a grid on a sheet of paper, Sunday through Saturday, seven spaces across and one o'clock a. m. till midnight of each day, twenty-four spaces down the page. After that, he had us fill in our required activities like our classes, personal maintenance, sleeping, eating, and working if we had jobs. In the empty spaces we found the time to study. Later I gave copies of this grid to all my students in every class I taught to help them find the time to write.

Actually, if you're like me, you'll need to practice lots of time management by making lists, using calendars, and retooling your schedule everyday. Life happens, you know?

Here are some examples of people I know who worked full time and still found the time to write.

One got up early and wrote from 5 a.m. till 7 a.m. before she left for work.

One went to work early to write on the office computer from 7 a. m. until 8:30 when his workday began.

A third drafted short stories during her lunch hour.

A fourth worked at his paid job ghostwriting articles for lawyers during the day at a coffee house. At home he worked on his novel from eight till ten at night.

Writers have had to do this sort of thing for centuries. For example, Nathaniel Hawthorne wrote in the morning before he trekked off to his job at the Custom House as "a weigher and gauger" of imported and exported goods.

4) Analyze your energy patterns and write when you're at your best.

You've probably heard the following: Some of us are owls, some larks. Try not to devote your best writing times to doing trivial things. If you're a lark, write in the morning, jog in the late afternoon when you need to get rid of the kinks that come from sitting and writing so much, and save the dishes to do at night when you're winding down.

5) Don't be inflexible. If you're a lark, but have an eight-to-five job, write at night.

6) PRIORITIZE. If writing is at the top of your daily to-do list, don't let dust bunnies, the baseball game on television, your daily exercise routine, or your quilting project interfere with your writing schedule.

PRIORITIZE: On the other hand, if baking cookies with your kid or grandkid is more important to you than drafting the third chapter of your novel, get out the baking tins and never look back. If, however, you long to write that wonderful novel based on the warm and kindly folks you knew when you grew up in Arkansas and those people keep walking into your mind and exhorting you to give them a world to live in, leave the baking tins in the cabinet and hit those keys.

Be aware that even after you've made a commitment to write, pretty often you'll have to reaffirm that commitment against the interruptions of someone running for office at the door or more likely on the phone. Speaking of the house phone, we still have one, but we usually keep the ringer off and the caller-blocked box is full.

I've discovered that I pretty much have to reset my priorities every day.

7) In spite of my earlier suggestions on this list, you might want to get the hard stuff out of the way first thing, so you don't waste time putting it off and risk not doing anything that day (or week).

For much of my indie author career, I've been uncomfortable with promoting my work. And I've lost many morning hours playing Solitaire on my cell phone, giving shout-outs to Facebook friends, cleaning out my email box, etc. to avoid touting my books. And then in the afternoon, I discover I really need to go to the grocery store and get some exercise, for crying out loud. And before I know it, it's five o'clock and I need to put supper on the table. For me, it's been pretty common that most days what I get done in the morning is what I end up getting done for the day. So recently, I've tried promoting in the mornings and writing in the afternoons to break that pattern. Sometimes it works. Sometimes it doesn't.

8) MAKE APPOINTMENTS TO WRITE AND KEEP THEM.

9) Solicit the cooperation of your family and friends in honoring your work time. One bribe is the promise of something dandy to read in a few weeks. But be willing to cooperate from time to time and let them drag you off to the family reunion. If you fuss too much, you'll get too upset to write anyway. You can take along your laptop and

revise a chapter or two on the sly. And just think. That old gal wearing the cotton housedress and pouring coffee from the huge, blue-enamel pot may be just the character your novel needs to resolve the conflict.

10) Make verbal contracts with your family members and friends. That is, tell them you're working on a great idea for a novel and that you plan on starting soon. Then you'll be embarrassed if you don't follow through.

Note: a side benefit of sharing your idea for a novel is your friends might contribute useful information like good research resources or even a joke that your protagonist might tell. Way back when I first started my humungous historical novel set in Ancient China, one of my friends told me she'd seen the cover of a book about daily life in Ancient China in the college library display case. I missed it because I didn't go to my office that way. But once I checked out the book, I found some wonderful information, especially pictures of artifacts.

Note: Avoid telling the whole plot of your novel in detail to your friends as you run the danger of talking out the story and thus not writing the novel at all.

11) Writing your novel is your long-range goal. Set short-range goals, too. Be specific. Say, for example, you figure the book you want to write will turn out to be about three hundred and sixty pages long. At an average of 250 words

a page, that's 90,000 words, and you'd like to finish the first draft in four months or 120 days. That turns out to be 22,500 words a month or 750 words a day every day of the week. That sounds quite doable, indeed, a fairly leisurely pace compared to NaNoWriMo's 1,667 words a day.

12) Give into any idiosyncrasies you might have instead of wasting time stewing about them. If you truly believe that writers, like artists, must starve in a garret, then rent an attic room, stock up on ramen, and never look back.

13) Don't wait around for your muse (aka your imp) to show up. Just get cracking on something, anything related to your novel. In other words, approach writing as a job, one very much worth doing. Writers often see little or no difference in quality between what they write when they're tired and cranky and a bit unwilling and what they write when they feel like they've got the world by the tail.

14) Personally, I've noticed that I waste a lot of time in my home office pawing through stacks of papers on my computer desk looking for things like notes for the next chapter or notes on how to do things like create book covers in Photoshop. So lately, I've tried to be more orderly about those things. I've got my instructions for making covers pinned to the corkboard behind me, and I try to file notes I've finished working with in my project notebook in my bookcase.

15) Efficiency experts say that you accomplish more if you give yourself regular breaks instead of trying to grind through a task hours at a time. So if you don't already have a fitness tracker, get one and set it to remind you to get up from your writing every hour and move around for a while.

At my advanced age, I've found that I can get into some serious pain if I sit too long. If I don't want that to happen, I must get up. And while I'm up, I usually get a drink of water. It's easy to get so caught up in a novel that you get really stiff and also dehydrated. While I'm up, I also might do a little chore, like folding clean clothes or going in the back yard and deadheading my petunias. In a pinch, I just dither in place by my computer desk. When my tracker says, "You crushed it!" I sit back down and resume typing. Positive reinforcement works really well to keep you going.

16) Be nice to yourself and reward yourself for your writing accomplishments.

I have this really bad habit of beating myself up at the end of the day for not doing each and every one of the nine or ten items on my to-do list. This can lead to depression. So I've decided to reward myself for time put in. And now, after I've put in a decent of time on some aspect of my writing career, I let myself check in with my Facebook friends on my phone or read some more of a friend's novel on my iPad mini.

Reaching bigger goals like creating your twenty cards calls for a bigger reward, like going out for supper at the pizza parlor close by.

Speaking of completing a major stage for writing your novel, now that I've discussed some things about time management, what comes next? Well, now you get to start working on your novel in earnest. Read on for some tips for drafting.

Tips on Drafting Your Novel

Originally, the scope of this book was for me to help you discover if you have a workable idea for a novel using twenty 3" by 5" index cards. But then I got to feeling that I'd be remiss if I didn't give you at least an overview of what it takes to draft a novel, that is, the basic process of drafting a novel with some tips along the way. So here's a sketch of that process along with this caveat: **The purpose of the first draft is to get to know your characters and tell yourself the story of your novel.**

1) Before you actually start drafting the novel, get acquainted with your characters at least a little bit because they are quite possibly the single most important element of your novel. I know from my experiences in my book club that most readers don't care much about novels this English major appreciates like a really well executed coming-of-age historical mystery set in New York City in 1919. If a reader doesn't like the characters, she might not like the book.

On the other hand, if readers love the characters, they might still love a novel that has a flaw or two. Several of the top novels or series among those on the list of *The Great American Read*, for example, have rather episodic plot lines. These include Diana Gabaldon's *Outlander* that came in as America's second favorite novel (after *To Kill a*

Mockingbird by Harper Lee), undoubtedly due to the charms of the resourceful time-traveling Claire and her stalwart man in kilts.

During the finale of *The Great American Read*, Gabaldon confided that when she first was working on *Outlander*, her husband discovered she had eighty files on her computer named *Jamie*. You might not want to do that much pre-writing about characters in your novel before you start working on it, but it will really help you if you explore them a bit.

Here are some methods you might use to get a handle on the characters you made several Novel Basics cards about.

Lots of people, including myself, use a set of basic questions they answer about each major character. My template includes the following: the character's name, his or her role in the book, gender, age, family and/or cultural background, basic physical appearance, usual manner of dress, distinctive physical feature and/or verbal habit. Also you might want to know the character's major psychological trait expressed in a single word, *ambitious* for instance. For mysteries, I also like to know each major character's secret.

Following the advice of science fiction/fantasy author Orson Scott Card in his book *Characters and Viewpoint,* part of Writer's Digest Books The Elements of Fiction Writing series, I keep a character bible for my cozy historical mysteries.

Sometimes you might let a character audition for the role you intend for her to have. That is, put your protagonist inside one of your obstacle scenes and see what she does and says.

Some writers will interview their characters up front. This is especially useful for the narrator of the story and also for the antagonist. (You might be surprised by what that villain has to say.)

Pin a picture of the character up on your corkboard if you have one. I modeled the Prince Charming of my Cinderella, P. I. fairy tale mysteries for grown-ups after Nathan Fillian–as Captain Mal in the *Firefly* series, not as Richard Castle later on. (Hey, it worked for me.)

2) As you draft, you might need to add additional characters, the chauffeur to drive the antagonist's limo in your thriller, for instance, or the snippy ladies maid who does your protagonist's hair in your Regency romance.

3) Remember those 5" by 8" cards I mentioned in the introduction? Now might be the time to get them out and use them for your scene cards. The bigger cards will give you room to jot down the important parts of each scene. Or you could create a template on a full 8½" by 11" sheet of paper that includes the basic elements of a scene. Or you can use both. Create the cards in the planning phase and the full sheets later when you write those scenes.

The big advantage of using cards at this point is you can move the cards around in a card file or on a corkboard before you commit to an order in your first draft. If you're using full sheets of paper, you can move them around in a notebook. I've done both. Both methods are easier than moving scenes around in your book after you've drafted it.

But before you start drafting, let's review the elements of a scene, the essential building block of fiction.

For one thing, a scene is structured like a novel with a clear beginning, middle and end. Often in fiction a scene begins with a character in a new place, and it covers a fairly limited part of the overall plot of the novel with a limited number of characters. It also takes a limited amount of time to play out.

At the start of a scene, the protagonist struggles to overcome one of the obstacles to achieving her goal. The attempt gets more and more tense until ultimately she fails. So she has to try again in another place or at a different time with possibly a different antagonist.

For instance, in *January Jinx*, the first novel in my Calendar Mystery series, Minty Wilcox answers several ads as she seeks to find a suitable job for a woman in Kansas City in 1899. Short scene by short scene, she enters a different office and talks with a different prospective boss. Each time she fails to get the position she's interviewing for. After an interval when she regains her strength and devises a new plan, she sets off again for another interview in another place.

As you plan the scenes of your novel, you will want to answer some basic questions for each one including these: Who's there? (It helps to have at least two characters so you can have dialogue and conflict.) Where and when does the scene take place? (This might include weather.) Do you want to include some specific object? (Consider the importance of Amy Dunne's diary in Gillian Flynn's *Gone Girl*.) Does the character succeed or fail to get what he or she wants by the end of the scene?

While we're on the subject of scenes, let me quickly lay out the five modes of discourse: dialogue, action, thought, exposition, and description. In a scene, you mostly use dialogue and action, and perhaps a bit of description at the start for a fast pace. Tip: In a scene, try to get your characters talking with each other and interacting fast. Save the thought and exposition, that is, explanation, for the slower paced segue between one scene and another. (We'll return to this topic later.)

Once you've figured out what your basic scenes will be, you have the skeleton of your novel. You might also want to go over all your obstacle cards and arrange them from the start of your novel until the end approximately in in order of intensity.

4) Once you've created cards or templates for at least your six major scenes and some of the others, you might want to plan your novel.

The planners among us like to prepare extensive outlines or lengthy synopses.

On the other hand, the pantsers among us love to go for it and see where they end up. They say an outline will spoil the spontaneity of the work and the process. The mother and son who write the Ian Rutledge historical mysteries as Charles Todd say they never know who the killer is when they start a new book. But be forewarned that even some highly experienced writers might never make it to the end of their novels if they don't know where they're going from the start.

Nancy Pickard, author of *The Scent of Rain and Lightning*, didn't outline the first few books in her Jenny Cain mystery series. Now she does. She says outlines ultimately save her time. But still she likes to write the first forty pages or so of a novel to see what she has before she commits to an outline.

As for me, I'm a planser, a hybrid of the planner and the pantser. For example, before I started writing that huge novel set in Ancient China, I only knew how I wanted the book to start and end, plus a dramatic game-changing scene in the middle. It worked out, but I did have to cut out parts that didn't work anymore and move other parts around.

Also earlier in my writing career, I resisted following the advice of Robert J. Ray, who says in his fine book *The Weekend Novelist*, that before you draft your novel, you should write the six major scenes starting with the first scene, followed by the last, the climax, midpoint, and the two plot point scenes. But for NaNoWriMo2018, I decided to take Ray's advice and at least sketch the six major scenes in the order he advises.

And you know what? I can see at least one great advantage in writing the first scene first and the last scene second, for example. Doing that, I got a much better sense of what characters and action that I would need earlier in the book, so I would know when and where to put them in place when I actually drafted the novel.

5) Make a quick sketch of your tentative cover that includes the title and your name or pseudonym. That's only right since often the cover sells your book or at least makes your potential reader hesitate and look again when she's scrolling through the "What's New" section of her favorite genre on Amazon.

Note: each genre has its own style of cover. The hard-boiled thriller with a male protagonist might feature the silhouette of some guy in a trench coat and slouch hat against the background of a famous London site soft with rain. A cozy mystery might feature a bright scene possibly with cats. (At one time, many novels featured original art pieces on their covers, but now cover-designers often use photographs of people and scenes put together in Photoshop.)

Titles of novels follow trends as well. For instance, the

names of mysteries especially tend to be brief, a single word or two. Keeping your title short is good no matter your genre. Dick Francis, whose novels featured protagonists engaged in some aspect of horse racing, chose many wonderful single word titles like *Shattered* about a glass blower who made the awards for horse races. Still, no one seems bothered by the six-word titles of the books in the Harry Potter series.

6) At this point I also suggest you tentatively shape your plot into chapters. Different authors have different ways of doing this. Some have many short chapters, each one a scene. Others have fewer but longer chapters, each one composed of several scenes that go together to create a major chunk of the plot.

I really like Dick Francis's style of shaping chapters in his horse racing thrillers. He began each chapter *in medias res*, that is, in the middle of a conflict, which he resolved with the protagonist probably failing. After a page break, he showed the protagonist recouping and setting off to try something different. After another page break, Francis began a new scene that he carried up to a really tense point where he ended that chapter, creating a cliffhanger that makes you just keep reading into the next chapter. Francis was very good at keeping his readers gripped by the plot.

7) I also suggest that you **Keep It** Simple, Student with

your novel, especially if it's your first, and avoid lots of flashbacks and shifts of point of view. Unless you're a really skilled, practiced writer, what might be easy for you to write ultimately might be hard for your reader to follow.

8) Another tip or suggestion: for some kinds of novels, you might need to do research before you start. For instance, every time I start the next book in my Calendar Mystery series that now includes the novels *January Jinx*, *Fatal February*, *Mischief in March*, and *Old Time Stories*, a collection of fiction and nonfiction, I go into the archives of *The Kansas City Star* and look at all the daily issues of the newspaper for the month and year involved in the book. I've done that also with the short stories like "Detectives' Honeymoon."

If you're writing a police procedural mystery, you might take a workshop on the subject or Google the heck out of it. You might also visit a police station and ride along with a police officer.

Science fiction writers like Andy Weir and my long-time favorite C. J. Cherryh need to know what they're talking about. Though fantasy authors often make lots of things up, Marie Brennan in her Lady Trent novels based her fabulous dragons on evolutionary science. Also be forewarned that you might need to do additional research during the process of writing your rough draft and after you've finished the rough draft.

Note: it's best to do your own research and not rely on

what you see on television shows and movies or the books you read. (One of my friends who wrote Regency Romance novels was surprised to see that the young ladies in similar books written by other authors frequented her fictional ladies' tailor shop Madame Cecile's.)

8) I'm paraphrasing Anne Lamott in *Bird by Bird*, her wonderful book on writing, when I pass on her advice to give yourself permission to write crappy first drafts.

9) On the other hand, do learn and use basic rules for punctuation, so you don't end up with hundreds of tiny glitches to fix when you've finished your draft.

Here's a rule especially useful for punctuating dialogue in American English usage. (It's different in the UK.) Commas and periods **always** go inside quotation marks. Colons and semi-colons **always** go outside quotation marks. Question marks and exclamation marks go inside or outside depending on the syntax of the sentence.

10) Also to save time, learn the shortcuts offered by your word processor. For instance, hitting the command key and the letter *P* on a Mac will bring up the print menu.

11) I format a novel for the print version from the start. This gives me a better idea of proportion and length of the book as it will eventually be.

12) Going back to the subject of chapters, instead of using one big long file for your novel, I like to put each chapter of a novel in a separate file until I'm about done with the book. That makes it easier for me to move chapters around if I need to.

13) Cultivate good stylistic writing habits such as employing showing writing instead of telling writing. (I'll say more on this topic later.) Doing so will lessen the amount of time you need to spend revising your novel.

14) Don't start rewriting your novel too soon because you'll probably just churn your wheels, miring yourself further and further in the same bog instead of making progress. (Reminder: we're not after perfection in the rough draft.) Indeed, John Braine in his book on writing novels suggests you finish the rough draft in as little time as possible (the thirty days of NaNoWriMo perhaps) and then take as long as you need to rewrite.

15) **Keep going.** If you haven't thought of a character's name yet, leave a blank, or use the character's role as a name like *Prot*, or use a placeholder name. I use *Whosit*. (I once called a male character "guy" in a standalone novel of suspense. And soon his name became Guy. Unfortunately, I can't do that again.)

Keep going. If you're not sure to how spell a word or

you know you'll need to do more research at some point or another, insert *TK* in brackets, a symbol suggested by a writer friend that I now use all the time to remind myself to check something later. (Use the Find and Replace command to find these quickly when you revise.)

Keep going. If you think of something you want to add earlier in your novel, describe the basic idea on a sticky note and slap it on your desk to place later on.

16) To help you get started as quickly as possible every time you write, finish each writing session by jotting down a short plan or outline of what you want to write next time. This can be especially important when you've just completed a chapter because often a new chapter is hard to start. Although I don't ascribe to Ernest Hemingway's practice of ending each writing session in the middle of a sentence, leaving off in the middle of some action works well for me.

17) Start each day's writing by looking over the previous day's installment either on paper or in your document file. I might make a quick edit and mark a few small things to fix later. But here's a warning. Do not rewrite passages over and over while you're doing the rough draft. Keep making progress in telling yourself the story of the book and getting to know your characters preferably day by day.

18) Try to foresee a problem in the plot enough in advance to "sleep on it." Say, for instance, if you know that in the next chapter, you'll get the hero into a snake pit, but you can't see how he'll escape, relax. Set it up as a problem for your imp to work on and forget it while you work on getting your protagonist into the fix. Chances are good that you'll wake up with the solution some morning soon. (You might have to make out a sticky note to set the solution up better earlier in the next draft.)

19) Let's talk about writer's block for a minute or two. I've come to realize that when I procrastinate about writing and do lots of trivial things like playing Solitaire on my phone, or–when I'm especially desperate, cleaning the slop out of the microwave–it might very well be a sign that I've taken a wrong turn in my novel recently. Lots of times when I go back a few pages, I find the problem, fix it, and then go back to where I stopped.

20) When you're in doubt about plot development, ask your characters. You can't let the antagonist kill the protagonist, but maybe you could let him come dangerously close. Seeing how your hero gets out of that fix can give you some good ideas. Or go back to the question you asked on the obstacle or wall card: What (else) could possibly happen?

21) A little warning: don't do so many preliminaries,

character sketches, etc. that you dissipate the energy you need to write the novel and never even start.

By now you might be getting restless with all the preliminaries. You might even be muttering, "Come on. When do I start writing my novel?" Peter Mathiessen says that writing a novel is simply a matter of gathering bits of information. When you have enough bits, you start writing the book. To me, you need to start drafting when your characters walk into your head in the middle of the night and talk to each other or to you. When you feel like you'll explode if you don't, you'd better start. But before you do, let's do a warm-up exercise.

Get something to write on and something to write with. Maybe you'll choose a pencil or pen and two or three full sized sheets of paper. Or you can use your laptop if you prefer. Get a timer or use the timer on your mobile phone. Set the timer for five to seven minutes.

Here's the basic rule for the exercise: Once you start writing, don't stop. Don't worry about spelling or correct usage. If you can't think of a name, leave a blank. If you get stuck, repeat the word you're stuck on until you think of something else to put on the page. Especially do not worry if you go off on a tangent from the topic you started with because you might discover what you really want to write about.

Here's the topic for this exercise: **Something that**

makes you really mad.

Ready. Set. Go.

When the time is up, finish the thought you're working on, put your pencil down or lift your hands from the keyboard. You might want to massage your hands as you think about what you just wrote, especially any surprises you noticed about what you wrote or how long it took to produce the number of lines you did.

Congratulations. You've just practiced sprint writing. I use this method a lot, especially when I draft my novels.

While you're gone, have fun getting to know your characters and telling yourself the story of your novel. And when you're done, come back, and I'll give some of the basics of rewriting it.

Oh, oh, I hear someone say. How long will I be gone?

That partly depends on you and how thoroughly you've brainstormed your novel before you start drafting. Danielle Steele, for instance, takes six months to research a novel and six months to rewrite, but she blasts through the rough draft in a month of crippling twenty-hour days. Ouch! That makes me tired. But lots of people now write 50,000 words in a month at the rate of 1,667 words a day.

Goodbye for now. We'll talk again on the other side.

PART 3: Rewrite Your Novel

An Overview of Revision
Rewriting for Improved Content
Getting Feedback
Rewriting for Improved Style
Rewriting for Correctness

An Overview of Revision

Congratulations! You've completed the first draft of your novel and the joy of creation still surges through your veins. You might even be on a bona fide writer's high induced by endorphins.

But don't rest on your laurels too long, for now you have to rewrite. No, I don't, you say. I just run the spell checker and shoot my novel off to an agent, right? That's probably a mistake because you might still be caught up in the fever of creation. Indeed, I've heard quite a few writers say that they wished they hadn't rushed too soon into submitting their novels to agents or publishing their novels themselves and, instead, taken the time to edit.

Personally, I usually heave a sigh of relief that I've made it to the end of my story and can relax a little bit because now I have something concrete to work with instead of a bunch of ideas banging around inside my head.

But some writers are filled with such disgust and loathing for the work when they complete their first draft that they're tempted to put the thing in the trash. Or they do. Or they put it in that drawer and never touch it again.

That really isn't a great way to respond either. In my experience as a writing instructor, I've found that most first drafts have elements that work quite well and others that need work. Stepping back from your novel will help you sort these out. Possibly you'll also think of new things to add to your book that might work.

So once you've completed your first draft, celebrate your accomplishment. And maybe do some chores around the house that you neglected while you wrote and wrote and wrote. After doing NaNoWriMo four times, I've learned to take the rest of the year off, or most of it anyway. You might want to do that, too. With the distractions of the holidays, you probably won't get too much done on your novel anyway.

But do come back to rewrite your novel in a timely fashion. Revision is a vital part of the process of writing, the part that "makes the work come alive," to quote Nancy Pickard, author of several popular mystery novels including Kansas Book of the Year, *The Virgin of Small Plains*. During rewriting, you re-envision the work and bring it closer to your original intention, obscured or lost in the heat of creating the rough draft.

Though often the writer comes up with new material during the rewriting phase, generally this last stage involves more analysis than creation, less the right side of the brain than the left. In other words, it's time for you to start listening more to your ump than your imp. While new writers often think they can't write unless they get it right the first time, most professionals rely on rewriting to bring their work up to par.

Okay, okay, I'm convinced, you say. So how many revisions should I do? As many as it takes, sweetheart. I hope that doesn't sound snotty. Many pros freely admit to doing up to twelve major revisions of their novels. Stephen King does two drafts–the second ten percent shorter than the first. The average romance author does two and a half to three drafts, but Nancy Pickard says that she rewrites virtually up to the day of publication.

But keep in mind that writers like King have the help of a professional editorial staff. As an indie author who does all the work of writing and editing myself, I average about six drafts for a novel. The initial rewrite takes quite a bit of time depending on how rough the draft turned out to be, but later drafts go faster and faster as I have less and less to tweak and fix.

Here are the basic methods you'll use to revise your novel: **cut**, **add**, **change**, **move**, and **combine**. But verily I say unto you, the greatest of these is **CUT**.

In rewriting, concentrate on these areas in this order: content, style, and mechanics. Why this order? you ask. Simple. It makes sense to get the content right before you spend hours polishing a sentence (paragraph, scene, chapter) that you might have to cut later–or worse, refuse to cut, though it no longer fits in the work, because you worked so hard on it.

On the other hand, if you're rewriting the content of your novel and notice a sentence you can improve quickly or an error to correct, go ahead. Similarly, if you think of a great new bit of dialogue in a later stage of revision, by all means add it. (But be sure to edit that material with special care.)

Rewriting for Improved Content

When you're ready to start rewriting your novel, be patient and don't just dive in, something I tend to do. Instead, read the novel through, maybe adding a few notes in the margin here and there like *develop* or *dev* for short if you notice skimpy places. (Tip: To do this on your computer if you use Microsoft Word, pull down the Insert menu and click on New Comment.)

Once you've read the novel through, go back and skim it, taking notes on what you see and patterns you notice. For instance, does your novel have a clear *Who wants what?"* established early. Does your protagonist clearly drive the plot car overall, but especially in the later parts?

In this pass, pay attention to the big issues of structure, that is, the skeleton of the book established by the six critical scenes. Does your novel have a first scene that hooks the reader? Do you have a scene near the end of Act 1 that leads to the major story line developed in Act 2? Is there some sort of important development about halfway through the novel? Is there a scene near the end of Act 2 that sets up Act 3? Does your novel have a tense and exciting climax and a satisfactory final resolution? If you can't find one of your vital six scenes, scout the draft to find a place to put it in your revision. Do some math to see where these important scenes fall in relationship to the overall length.

Consider your narrative line. Once you start your story, do you continue in a straightforward chronological line or do you switch back and forth in time, from past to present to future to past? Think about your audience and this maxim: the larger the market you want for your novel, the easier you want to make your novel to read. That matters especially when you're writing popular fiction. A professional editor once scolded me for having too many flashbacks in the first part of one of my novels, so I took most of them out.

Consider the type of novel you're writing and reader expectations for that genre. If you're writing a categorical romance, for instance, do you have at least one love scene? If you're writing a mystery, is there a body or at least a crime?

On the basis of your observations, prepare an outline or write a narrative synopsis. Tip: Do not consider your outline or synopsis as carved in stone.

To set up the next section, let me remind you of the modes of discourse:

Dialogue

Action

Thought

Exposition

Description

The balance of these modes depends in part on the genre of your novel, the age of your intended reader, and your intended effect on the reader of your book. A fast-paced thriller, for instance, will rely mostly on dear old **DAD**, that is, dialogue and action with a bit of essential description here and there though probably at the start of a scene, so you don't slow down the action later on. Literary novels will include more **TED**, that is, more thought, exposition and description.

As you write a second draft and concentrate on content, you might want to **CUT**

1) all or part of ground clutter (action that leads nowhere),

2) sections of dialogue that run on too long,

3) unneeded characters and everything related to them,

4) sections of description that run on too long (one perfect detail is better than three okay ones),

5) scenes that contribute only slightly to the plot,

6) extended sections of background or exposition,

7) unneeded transitions between scenes,

8) sections that tell the reader what to think instead of letting them draw their own conclusions,

9) unneeded or overlong passages of thought,

10) unneeded material between the second set-up scene and the climax,

11) and any element that impedes the pace.

(I'm chuckling as I type because of the length of this list. Please don't let it intimidate you. Just take your time and enjoy revising your novel.)

On the other hand, instead of cutting much, some authors draft short and revise long, as if they were blowing up a balloon. Even if you don't follow their example, you still might need to **ADD**

1) elements and details that set up plot developments you didn't know about when you wrote earlier parts of the book,

2) descriptions to make characters or settings come alive,

3) character motivations,

4) background information,

5) more dialogue,

6) significant action,

7) reminders to the reader,

8) foreshadowing and/or clues and red herrings,

9) symbols and metaphors to highlight theme,

10) transitions between scenes,

11) and surprises! (All readers enjoy those.)

Often you will want to **CHANGE** elements, for instance, from telling writing into showing writing. What's the difference? you might ask.

Here's a sample. Telling writing: The room looked cozy. Showing writing: On the far side of the room, a crackling fire on the hearth cast flickering light on two chairs piled high with cushions. The wind howled savagely against the frosted window as he crossed the room, past the chairs. Bending down, he held his stiff fingers toward the warmth of the flames. Ah, that feels good, he thought.

Note how many more details appear in the revised version. God is in the detail in writing fiction, that's for sure.

Note also the use of direct thought in the revision and how it's punctuated like dialogue but without quotation marks.

In revising, author Nancy Pickard checks her scenes to make sure they contain details that appeal to all five of our senses: sight, sound, smell, taste, and touch.

You might also want to shift from indirect speech to direct. Indirect speech: he told her about the game, but she wasn't interested. Direct speech: "Wow," Bob said. "You should have been there, Susie."

"I don't care about that stuff," Susie said.

Tip: For economy, that is, to say the most in the fewest words, use dialogue lots because dialogue does at least two things at once including

1) present action going on at the moment,
2) present background from the past,
3) describe characters and settings,
4) develop character,
5) express emotion,
6) create suspense,
7) and most important of all, play out conflict.

Dialogue breathes life into your characters and your

novel. Use it often.

Something that writers sometimes do in a revision is change the viewpoint of the narrator. For instance, Linda Rodriguez said that once she changed the perspective of narrator in her first Skeet Bannion mystery from third person to first person–that is, from *she* to *I*–the character and the book really came alive for her.

Sometimes, too, you might find that, in drafting, you got in a rush and tried to do everything at once. So in revising, you might need to **MOVE**

1) exposition from early in the novel, scene or chapter, to later on,

2) exposition closer to the action it relates to,

3) and thematic commentary or epiphanies closer to the end.

You might also need to move scenes and chapters, and plot points. Something I've done and I'm not alone in that, is try to introduce too many characters at once at the start of a book. So you might want to move some characters from early in the book to later on.

Finally, you might need to **COMBINE** one character with another or one scene with another.

Getting Feedback

Once you have the content of your novel about right and can think of nothing much else to do with it–this might take more than one draft–let some gentle people read your novel and do something that you absolutely can't do for yourself: **tell you what it's like to read your novel for the first time**. (Thanks to author Orson Scott Card for this tip.)

Where can you find those readers? In a variety of places, but one element is crucial. **Whoever you choose must be familiar with your book's genre because they read that kind of book all the time and possibly because they also write in the genre.** Thus they will recognize the conventions of that sort of book and respect its intention.

Some of you reading *Novel Basics* might have an agent and/or an editor at a publishing house from previous projects who will read your new work. Other writers at your publisher might read Advanced Review Copies (aka ARCs) as well. But if you're just starting out or an indie author, you won't have this sort of reader. So here are some places to look.

1) Some writers share their drafts with family members. Stephen King's wife, for instance, saved an early draft of *Carrie* from the trash where he'd thrown it.

2) You might have a friend who reads and/or writes in the same genre as you do.

3) Writers groups can be helpful. Still, if most of the

other writers in your group write poetry or nonfiction themselves, they might not be so familiar with fiction, let alone the kind of novel you're writing.

4) A better choice of where to look for readers might be members of a specific group related to your novel's genre. Examples include Romance Writers of America, the Historical Novel Society, the Society of Children's Book Writers and Illustrators, Mystery Writers of America, and Sisters in Crime. The latter has an on-line writing group for newbies called Guppies that some of my fellow mystery writers have gotten lots of help from.

5) Many of my Facebook friends also write cozy mystery fiction. And from time to time some of them send out requests for readers in exchange for ARCs. You might follow suit.

6) You can hire what's called a developmental editor to read your novel and give you feedback. Perhaps a writer friend can recommend an editor of this kind to you. You can find many prospective editors online, but many of those offers are scams. Tip: if they ask for money up front, move on. If you find one with a reliable track record and the price is within your budget, this choice might work for you.

<> <> <>

Here are some tips and suggestions for getting the most out of this part of the writing process. Please note that what you really need at this point in the process is **feedback on what works in your novel and what needs work overall.**

Before you submit your work to readers,

1) don't explain what you were trying to do since they'll give you feedback only on that aspect;

2) don't apologize since that might provoke either a "there, there, it's really good" response or a brutal slam: "This is the worst piece of crap I've ever read";

3) do set up clear expectations of what you want from your readers;

4) make it clear you don't want or need proofreading right now. I've had readers who quibbled about my punctuation, grammar, and word choices. They were wrong, of course. Still, this type of reader spends all his time or her efforts on the little stuff instead of giving feedback on elements you need help with like the larger elements of characterization, plot structure, pace, balance of modes and so on;

5) if you have a question about some part of your novel, ask it at the end of your manuscript in a little note instead of asking it at the start because again your readers might only look for that;

6) if you want to, invite your readers to make suggestions of what might work though sometimes this provokes an "if this were my novel, I'd . . ." response that probably won't be helpful.

When you get your novel back from your readers, look over their comments and rewrite to improve the content at least one more time.

You might get a range of opinions, depending on how many readers you had. Look especially for consensus instead of the outliers on either end: your aunt Edith who heaps the highest praise on your novel because she's very proud that you can even string three words together and likes to brag to her friends about you, or the jerk who completely slams your work to demoralize you on the theory that the less competition the better, right? (Wrong!)

You might also run into the self-proclaimed expert who says that you chose absolutely the wrong kind of saddle for the steed belonging to the hero of your Regency romance. (This happened to a writer friend of mine.) The reader's probably wrong, but check it out if you're uncertain. (But don't waste your precious time getting into an argument over the issue with this sort of person.)

4On the other hand, you might receive a lovely little nugget of a detail from a reader that you can use in your novel. For example, one of my friends told me that her grandfather brought lumber into Kansas City in the late 19th century on a wagon pulled by oxen. I had lots of fun with that wagon interfering with my heroine's search for an abducted friend in *January Jinx*, the first book in my historical mystery series. (Note: get permission up front to use someone else's juicy detail in your book and thank them in your acknowledgements at the end of your novel.)

Once the content seems about right, move on to the next phase of rewriting. Advice: At this point, it's good to put all your chapters into a single file, so you can also spot glitches in formatting for your eBook or POD versions of your novel as you edit.

Rewriting for Improved Style

Verily, again I say unto you, the greatest of your tools is **CUT**. Overall, including cuts for both content and style, follow Stephen King's example and try to make your final version at least ten percent shorter than earlier drafts. Some writers draft very long and cut out nearly half.

For concision, **CUT**

1) redundancies;

2) one, two or even three adjectives out of every three;

3) *there is/are, which is/are, it is . . . that*;

4) excessive or elaborate dialogue tags;

5) and most adverbs.

For clarity and coherence, you might need to **ADD** transitions and dialogue tags.

For clarity, vitality and ease of reading, **CHANGE**

1) long sentences and paragraphs into shorter ones, especially in action scenes;

2) long words into shorter ones;

3) jargon into everyday words;

5) over-used words into less common words;

6) **passive voice into active voice** (instead of *The boy was hit by a car*, say, *The red Beamer struck the toddler and sped away.*)

7) state of being verbs into action verbs (instead of *He's an active kid*, say *Ronnie buzzed into the room, ran in place for three seconds, and turning, raced back out again*);

8) progressive verbs into straight present or past tense (Instead of *He was running late that day*, say *He ran late that day*);

9) general into specific (instead of *cat*, say *a slinky black cat with yellow almond eyes and one white whisker*); abstract into concrete; unclear pronouns into nouns; and fuzzy word choices into just the right words.

For clarity and variety, occasionally **MOVE** phrases from their usual spots into more unusual ones. For example, *Occasionally **MOVE** phrases from their usual spots into more unusual ones for clarity and variety.*

For coherence and variety, occasionally **COMBINE** many short sentences into longer ones and many simple sentences into compound or complex ones.

Before you're done rewriting your novel, I highly recommend that you run an overall style checker. Here's how to do that with Microsoft Word. Go to the Preferences menu > Authoring and Proofing Tools > Grammar menu, and click on *Show readability statistics*. The document for *Novel Basics*, for example, has 2% passive voice (higher than my usual fiction percentage of 0%), 67.2% Flesch Reading Ease (considerably lower than my usual fiction reading ease of 85%), and 8.3 Flesch-Kincaid Grade Level. (No, I'm not related to that Kincaid.)

In contrast, the stories and novels in my Cinderella, P. I. fairy tale mysteries for grown ups that feature a favorite heroine twenty years, three years and a few extra pounds after the ball, average about the 3.5 grade level because I write them in first person perspective. I write my historical mystery series set in Kansas City around 1900 in third person, so the grade levels average from 4.1 to 5.2 grade levels.

Generally in fiction, I use short, everyday, yet specific and concrete words, so they average 4.1 characters. Because I use lots of dialogue, my paragraphs average around two sentences each. But I get in trouble with my sentences that can run on and on and on; they're perfect grammatically because when I was in Miss Sweetland Oxley's College Prep Senior English class at Huntington High School, from time to time we had to diagram sentences on the blackboard; but my long sentences tend to wear the reader out (by now you probably see what I mean); so something I always do in revising is hack those longer sentences up. Whew!

Rewriting for Correctness

What's the big deal about correctness? Won't the reader forgive me for a few errors here and there because really my novel is dynamite? Probably not. Instead they very well might run up to you when they see you at a party and say, "I read your book. You left out some words."

You can hire a copy editor if you have the money. But if you're a complete do-it-yourselfer like I am, you'll have to edit your novel yourself. (Some of my author friends shudder with horror when I tell them I edit my own work.) So edit with extreme care because mechanical errors and misspellings disrupt a reader's experience of your novel. They might also betray you as an amateur to agents, editors and readers.

No matter how sharp your editorial skills, always proofread your material several times before you submit it to an agent or an editor or before you publish it yourself. As a writing instructor, I've had over thirty-five years of editing experience, and I can spot a dangling modifier at twenty paces. But like many writers, I still miss stuff in my own writing like *t8his* or a crazy autocorrect like this one that appeared on Facebook: *top right* instead of the *too tight* I meant to say.

Here are some other suggestions.

1) You can and should use a spell checker, but still proofread for confused homonyms like "too," "to," "two."

2) If you don't know how to spell, learn. (The

community college where I taught for twenty-five years offers free spelling courses.)

3) If you don't know how to punctuate, take a review course, possibly available on line or in the writing center of your closest community college.

4) You might find it helpful to read your manuscript aloud. (James Michener and his editor read one of Michener's big novels to each other five times.) Chances are good you might catch the most common error of all that's really pesky to notice, dreaded omitted word. If you noticed that I need *the* before *dreaded*, good for you.

I once had a student in Composition 1 making *D*'s on his essays because of the many mechanical errors in his work. But then he began reading his papers out loud word for word backwards so he could catch the mistakes. He made a *B* in the course.

5) If you're editing a printout, run a ruler down the page line by line to slow you down, so you're more likely to notice errors. Mark the error in red to fix on the computer later. When you're editing on the screen, run the cursor down the right side of the text to help you find errors.

6) Currently, I use a track pad that sometimes highlights and moves a passage or even deletes the whole thing without my even noticing. So I try not to get in too much of a hurry in editing. Instead if I've changed anything on a page, I try to reread it on the screen before I move on to the next page.

7) It's also good, at some point or another in editing, to use the Find and Replace command to locate your personal trouble spots. (One of mine is over-using the word *then*.) Depending on your prospective reader, you might also want to check for certain word choices: profanity in sweet romances and cozy mysteries, for instance.

8) Sometimes my memory fails me. For instance, in the paragraph above I needed to stop and think about where the period should go–before or after the closing parentheses? It's good to have a reliable grammar handbook for those times. (I use a print copy of *A Pocket Style Manual* by Diana Hacker.)

9) If you write historical fiction as I do, you might want to use Google Books Ngram Viewer, a truly nifty tool a friend put me on to, to check for anachronisms among my word choices. For my historical mysteries, for instance, I have mine set to check for phrases in use between 1890 and 1900. It's less useful for single words. (For that, I use a dictionary called *American Slang* by Robert L. Chapman.) Still, the other day, I typed three nouns meaning the same thing into the Ngram Viewer to find out which one people most commonly used during the period of my work-in-progress.

10) Many times in my own work and in the published work of my friends, I see errors in whatever sections we have worked on most recently. So **always** take yet another look at those areas of your novel before you send it off or

publish it yourself.

There's a lot involved to the editing process. Be patient and take your time.

The Importance of Proofreading

As Jack Riley topped the final rise before town, he saw the buzzards circling above him. Not this time, he thought, a half smile on his face. He had just been through eighty miles of the roughest dessert anywhere.

The End

Dear Reader,

I hope you enjoyed this book and have gotten useful guidance for brainstorming, drafting, and revising your novel, whether it's your first or the most recent of several.

If you did find this book helpful, I'd truly appreciate it if you would review the book on Amazon and/or Goodreads. You don't need to write at length. Instead, you could rate the book and add a few words about which card or piece of advice you found especially helpful and why.

Editing is a long and painstaking task, and even the most experienced writer can get in a hurry and make mistakes. So if you noticed a glitch in this book, please email me at jkwryter@gmail.com and tell me about it, so I can fix it. I really appreciate any help you give me.

Also when you finish your novel, please me know by email at jkwryter@gmail.com, on Twitter where I'm JulietKincaid or on Facebook where I'm juliet.kincaid and JulietKincaidauthor2016, so I can congratulate you. I'm so excited for you.

All the best, Dr. J

About the Author

Juliet Kincaid has a life long passion for fiction, especially stories and novels that provide adventure and escape. Mystery, fun, and romance help, too. Juliet believes that laughter is the best medicine for pretty much whatever ails you. And so she gives her books and stories happy endings because life provides so few of them.

Juliet's published work includes a series of cozy historical mysteries that tell the story of a smart business girl and a dashing detective in Kansas City, a place that could get downright deadly a hundred years or so ago; and the Cinderella, P. I. fairy tale cozy mysteries for grown-ups that feature a favorite heroine twenty years, three kids and a few extra pounds after the ball. (Happy endings guaranteed!)

To learn more about Juliet's publications, subscribe to her website at www.julietkincaid.com or go to her Amazon Author Central page at https://www.amazon.com/Juliet-Kincaid/e/B00DB4HWRG

If you're interested in having Juliet speak to your book club on the importance of reviewing the novels you all love or present her Novel Basics class to your writers' group (in the Greater Kansas City Metro area), contact her at jkwryter@gmail.com.